Days and Nights
of
Game Fishing

Days and Nights
of
Game Fishing

W. B. Currie

Illustrations by Charles Jardine

UNWIN HYMAN
London   Sydney

First published in Great Britain by George Allen & Unwin 1984
This paperback edition first published by Unwin Hyman,
an imprint of Unwin Hyman Limited, 1987

UNWIN HYMAN LIMITED
Denmark House, 37–39 Queen Elizabeth Street
London SE1 2QB
and
40 Museum Street, London WC1A 1LU

Allen & Unwin Australia Pty Ltd.
8 Napier Street, North Sydney, NSW 2060, Australia

Allen & Unwin New Zealand Ltd. with the Port Nicholson Press
60 Cambridge Terrace, Wellington, New Zealand

British Library Cataloguing in Publication Data

Currie, William B.
   Days and nights of game fishing.
1. Salmon-fishing – Great Britain 2. Fly
fishing 3. Trout fishing – Great Britain
I. Title
799.1'755   SH684
ISBN 0–04–799038–4

Set in 11 on 13 point Garamond by
Nene Phototypesetters Ltd, Northampton
and printed in Great Britain by
Butler & Tanner Ltd, Frome and London

Acknowledgements

A fishing book of this sort draws on a very wide range of stimulus material – river and lochside discussions, the advice (and disagreement) of ghillies and boatmen, and all manner of sources of what makes up fishing and its discourse. I would like to acknowledge these influences, over more than four decades of active angling and to thank all my friends and colleagues for their interest and help. I should also like to thank the editors of certain angling magazines not only for giving me a forum for writing about my sport but for allowing me to publish material in this book which directly reproduces part or all of certain articles they have published. Specifically, I would like to thank Mr Roy Eaton, *Trout and Salmon*, for allowing me to use *Demythologising Mishnish* and *Hooking Salmon on the Fly* which appeared in his magazine under different titles. I should also, in the same way, like to thank the Editor of *The Field* for permission to use *Big Day at Boleside* and *The St Andrew's Day Event*, and Crawford Little, for permission to use *Night Sea Trout – a Revised Manifesto* and *The Essence of Tweed in Autumn*, which appeared in *Countrysport*.

WILLIAM B. CURRIE
Edinburgh, 1984

Contents

ix

─── Introduction ───

There is a convention, amounting almost to a conspiracy, that anglers writing about their sport should keep reminiscence down to a minimum. Yet, thinking back on several decades of fishing and reading about it, not to mention writing about it, I find fresh in my memory splendidly reminiscent books about the sport – Negley Farson's *Going Fishing*, Sir Robert Bruce Lockhart's *My Rod My Comfort*, George Brennan's *Halycon Days*, A. R. B. Haldane's *The Path by the Water*, and many others. I think the convention of not telling your story is based on two fears: first, that the story itself will be dreary, like one of those club tales told by the equivalent of The Ancient Mariner who holds you with his glittering eye, bores the tail off you, and makes you wish you had forgone the pleasure of it all; second, wariness of reminiscence may stem from a justifiable caution over nostalgia, which, in its extreme form, can become a special kind of lie.

I think also we are in a period of what might be called the development of leisure and those who publish books and magazines about fishing are quite rightly conscious of helping people to take up the sport, to develop their fishing skills and to broaden their horizons. To some, fishing instances do not add up to a good fishing perspective; no amount of reminiscence about taking salmon on the floating line on the Dee will teach the skill to others. There is, however, a red herring of considerable size in this view. Any teacher knows how effective a good example is and, at least in fair proportion, telling your story at the right moment can be highly effective and can make the learning memorable.

Recalling fishing days when things went right might make people think that Currie's days were all like that, and a completely misleading view of the writer's luck might emerge. Worse still, a reader might think that, unless his fishing matches the one-off brilliance of a lucky day which the author recalls, his own sport is somehow inferior. There is, I think, a very important point here for all writers on the sport. The day of great success, or the unusual event, can only have value if it is set against the normal failures we all experience. I have experienced fishing where catches were easy, inevitable and maximum, but if this were the norm it would be so boring that I would want to give up the sport altogether.

So this book is about fishing days but it is not a diary. It is, partly, I hope, about the feelings, the challenges and the deep compulsions of going fishing for salmon, sea trout and trout. It deals with territory and much-loved places within it and with the way water links all this together into a special perception of one's native land. It is also, and perhaps principally, a book about the joy of it all. Writing about one's fishing days in these terms is, of course, writing about part of one's life; it is an *apologia pro vita sua*. I know that fishing is not itself a reason for living, but I would find a life devoid of it seriously diminished.

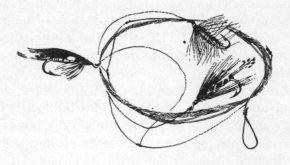

⊣ I ⊢

A Salmon Fisher's Apology

I do not really understand the compulsions of salmon fishing, but I am well aware that I am gripped by them. Looking forward to a good day's salmon fishing can still keep me awake the night before, turning over the possibilities in my head and wondering whether my hooks are sharp enough. Why should this be, thirty-seven years after catching my first salmon and with all manner of catches to report for my efforts? The urge to fish for salmon is quite unlike the urge to fish for trout. Trout fishing is much more reasonable, more logical and in every way a more delicate art. After all, when we think our way into a day's trout fishing we are weighing up the tactics for a resident fish which feeds because it is hungry, which has a recent degree of wildness and wariness and which can be pursued relatively inexpensively in attractive weather. Salmon do not feed in fresh water, although they do have feeding reflexes, of which little is understood; they are migratory, coming from incredible distances at sea to our rivers; they can be extremely stupid fish, easier to catch, on rare occasions, that the cuddies we caught off west-coast piers as children; they are expensive fish to pursue, and at least half of the season falls in weather which is far from idyllic.

It would perhaps be better if I gave no explanation for wanting so much to fish for salmon. I don't think I want to know what Freudians would say about it; nor will it help to be told again that salmon fishing is a branch of idealism, a longing for the impossible satisfactions of a non-existent world. I certainly never want to add up the days and hours I have spent fishing for salmon, and I absolutely refuse to calculate what this has cost in terms of diverted energies and empires which might have been built with the same application. I prefer to handle it another way. I have wallowed in my fishing, salmon, sea trout and trout, not for a score of years, like Donne's repentant sinner, but for something like twice that time. It has given me enormous pleasure, and a great deal to think about. Surely I can transmit something of that in place of an explanation?

It happens like this. I used to have one Saturday a fortnight on Burnbane, an interesting if not particularly distinguished beat on middle Tay. It is really a spring water, with sport up to the middle of June and with a burst of great activity in September and early October. During the summer, however, the Tay brings in pockets of fish, sometimes grilse and sometimes much heavier salmon. You never know if they are there or not, until you hook a fish and find that it is very far indeed from a resident, stale springer, but is everything a clean-run salmon should be. I used to fish Burnbane as often as I could with fly and when the river fell to its bare bones in summer fly became tremendous fun. The great unbroken glides of the Tay, in the lowest water, defined themselves as streams with lies, deep and shallow pockets, vee shelters and everything productive salmon water should have. The glides which seemed slowish in high water got faster in low conditions, possibly because the pools below had lower levels and allowed more pronounced gradients in the streams.

There is a pool called Sparrowmuir on Burnbane which is really the extended tail of the Caputh Bridge Pool above our beat and it has, well in towards the left bank, a little heap of boulders which forms the most attractive fast vee in low conditions. To fish it well, you have to wade in from the right bank, over shingle and round stones, and to cover the lie well you have to go as deep as you dare, leaning against the weight of the Tay as it pours down. I found myself doing this one Saturday in early July under a bright sky. I was fishing a size 6 double Claret Shrimp, which you will possibly not find in regular catalogues of salmon flies, because it was a variant tied up by a friend of mine. To fish a fast vee like this, with a long line, you have to get the fly somehow to hang as it passes the fish, and this means a long line out, a high top and a mend. I tried a couple of times and the fly merely pulled quickly off the lie because of the weight of water on the line. I waded a yard further out, risking a ducking, cast again and got it right. As the fly came over the lie, which was hard in to my side of the vee, there was a sudden bulge on the water, a heavy pull, and I was into a fish which immediately turned downstream and, using all the force of the Tay, stripped line and backing off the reel in a great rush. I established contact properly and edged my way out of the river, got on to the shingle and then, as quickly as I could, got down to the basin below where the fish had stopped. It was a hard but reasonable fight from that point on, and it was not too long before I saw him, gleaming in the water. Fast fish, like this one, often come in easily at the end of the fight. This splendid fish did and I tailed him out on to the shingle, an absolutely splendid 15½-pounder with sea lice on.

I did not wait. I went in again and with a rather breathless urgency repeated the approach and had the enormous satisfaction of taking a fourteen-pounder from the same lie. These were marvellous chance fish. What a pair they made! I looked at them on the clean sunlit shingle, sat down beside them and looked at the place and the day and the optimistic sky above Perthshire. Words cannot really convey the sense of achievement I felt then, and recapture now. It was some kind of existential moment at the very heart of the sport.

Fish which you remember are not necessarily the large ones. In my penniless student days I used to go up to Caithness and

fish not very productive beats of the Thurso river, but, because I was there and was slightly daft, I would be given the stormy hail-lashed ends of some afternoons to fish when a tenant of a better beat gave up and was kind enough to ask me to fish for him. Quite often nothing happened, but from time to time a fish would take my fly in weather which had driven reasonable men indoors. I recall fishing the stream into Loch Beg on beat 15, as it then was, and getting nothing at first until I tied on my biggest Waddington, let it sink well into the loch and walked it back up the stream. A fine clean eight-pounder took it and was duly presented to the tenant at the Ulbster Arms. That, incidentally, was perhaps my first salmon taken by 'backing up', a technique which I use extensively when I fish rivers in the north – Helmsdale, Thurso and other waters with quiet reaches lacking in stream.

Memorable fish are not necessarily large, nor are they always fresh, shining salmon, pictures of beauty. I was trout fishing the Doon in Ayrshire one hopeless low summer day on that interesting but not spectacular beat, Smithston, at the head of the Boreland Glen where the river is a pattern of shallow streams, large boulders and pot-holes. I was not doing well. The trout were not interested and no finnock seemed to be in the water. Then a small, red salmon splashed in a pot-hole below me. I changed my tail fly to a half-inch Stoat's Tail tube fly with a small treble, wet it and covered the pot. I thought I had drawn a blank, quite a usual thing when you are trying in low summer water for a splashing fish. Then like a flash I was into him. In low, stony water like that, fish have no water to run through and fight in. This fish did not seem to notice that there was nothing

4

to swim in. It moved over thin shingle, walloped behind stones and showed for more than half the fight. It was, as I said, not in any way a spectacular fish. It weighed five pounds, was red, and slightly thin. But what a catch! I crowed over it and remember it long after days of multiple fat salmon on fine pools of Tay and Tweed have been forgotten.

Catching salmon, sea trout and trout is for me always something of a learning experience. I honestly do not know the inside story of why fish take. With trout, my predictions are often straightforward: fish are feeding on, say, small sedges on a loch on a July evening, so I fish a sedgy pattern in a sedgy way and kill several. With sea trout I can often predict places they will take the fly in the dark and in many cases it works out. Sometimes salmon seem to respond to what you have learned about them, but there are many occasions when everything seems right but no fish take. You run through the possibilities, change tactics, try to equate the conditions with something similar you have coped with, and still get nothing. Then a fish takes you, astonishingly, but very welcome. In your mind the question is formed: 'What on earth did I do right?' I believe that learning about salmon is somehow twigging what went right when all your predictions were wrong. For me that is a learning experience of some note. You are face to face with your own ignorance, and with the nearly impenetrable mystery of what is actually going on under the surface of the river. There is a sense in all this of communicating with the salmon in its own special world and making sense of the messages you get. Writing about the experience is an attempt to pass on the events and the ideas which come one's way. There is, therefore, a triple goal, as I have written elsewhere, and it is best expressed in the rules once laid down for the criticism of poetry: *ut doceat*, that it should teach; *ut moveat*, that it should stir the reader; and *ut delectet*, that it should add to the beauty of experience. Salmon, sea-trout and trout fishing do all three for me and my goal in writing about game fishing is to transmit all three aspects of the sport to those who read about it.

———◄ 2 ►———

Helmsdale Februaries

The Helmsdale in February should not be thought of as a paradise full of fish. Paradise it may be but in the first weeks of the season it is a very different river from the Helmsdale of summer full of eager fresh fish after a little rain. In February the Strath of Kildonan is magnificent, sometimes snow-covered, almost always wind-swept. It is a desolate, serene valley with what appear to be endless heathery moors backed by substantial hills rolling to the north and the south. It can be the coldest and most inhospitable valley when gale-force north-easters blow straight up the glen from the North Sea, sometimes bringing winds so strong that you can hardly hold a rod up as you fish. Yet February on the Helmsdale can produce mild days of picnic weather – far more, in my experience, than March produces. It can present you with a singing sort of landscape where you can almost hear the whole riverside stirring itself, rejecting the bonds of winter and getting ready to embrace the spring.

The river itself is a remarkable water, but you might make many mistakes about it as you give it a casual glance. It is a small water in a short valley, flowing only twenty-five miles from its main headwater in the Badanloch. In spring it is an even shorter water since it is effectively halved by the falls of Kildonan and spring fish are normally caught below this point. Perhaps it was with this in mind that the proprietors who originally designed the fishery there divided the fishing beats into upper and lower, and you have an option of fishing your numbered beat above or below the falls. In February your chance of a springer is on the lower river, even if a small number of fish may have run the falls as early as that. I have watched February fish running the falls but I do not know of any fish taken on the upper river much before April.

February on many rivers is a month of heavy water, especially in a black February which brings down water from the melting snows on the hills behind. Sutherland does not hold much snow. Its main mountains are in the west of the county, under the influence of the mild winds blowing off the Gulf Stream. You will, of course, see snow many times in the strath in February – and in March and sometimes in April – but it will tend to be short-lived, piling down on you one day, lying around wetly the next, and gone the third. Some years do bring heavier snow, of course, but we have lost comparatively few fishing days over the past years either because of roads being blocked by snow or rivers full of cold melt-water.

It is much more typical to have to deal with ice on the Helmsdale in February. Sheet ice is very common. It forms during the night and can close off slow pools in a few hours of hard frost. This is a problem, but not a desperate one because ice can be broken off pools. The more difficult problem is grue, which can ruin fishing. Grue is the name given to ice crystals forming in the running water. When the temperature of the flowing water falls to freezing-point, clusters of ice crystals form in little blobs in the water. Blob joins with blob and forms anything from a pattern of floating ice crystals hardly visible as they bob gently down the glides to a mass of ice, deep and dense, rustling over the stones and jamming in the narrows. It hisses at you as the river moves it; it shows everywhere, sometimes forming a slowly jostling and heaving mass with lower grue pushing the top layers into the air in small menacing movements. Ice can also form on the river bed in masses, making the water change colour, in the case of the Helmsdale to

7

a yellowish cold liquor. When grue comes, fishing is impossible. The remedy? Quite simply to wait for the water to heat up
even to half a degree above freezing-point, when the water will
clear itself as you watch and experienced anglers fish hard,
because the going of the grue is an excellent time to take a fish
on the fly.

I have got into fish several times just as the grue has
disappeared. One particular February day comes to mind. I was
fishing on beat 2 with its fine rocky pools and, at the lower
extremity of the beat, the massive open pool of Kilfedir. I
walked up through a grove of birches above Kilfedir along
banks with whins and sandy bluffs and boulders. I tried the
half-dozen casts in Johnny Gordon's Pool, a small, productive
neck of water in a basin of rock. Nothing there but grue still
clinging to my flies. Then to the Gate Pool above, sometimes a
memorable and wild place for spring salmon. Nothing. The
Gate looked magnificent in the lowish water. The river forms a
small island at the head and turns on the right bank almost at
ninety degrees to rush across the higher bank opposite and turn
down to form a deep, rocky run with lies which in propitious
times I have seen full of February fish. The grue was nearly off,
by now, and you could feel the change. There was a breath of
spring in the air, which being translated into cold scientific fact
probably meant that the air temperature had risen a couple of
degrees above freezing and the water was following it. I walked
up the open grassy field to the Park above and there, in a pool
which has sometimes been a very generous one to me in spring,
I saw the last of the grue go. My two-inch Brora fly – a Willie
Gunn dressed with a mixture of yellow, black and red hair over
a black, gold-wound body – fished well and, out over the main
stream, in a lie I know well, I had a pull. It was not the bottom. It
kicked, turned downstream, and turned back into the fast water
below me.

You know what runs through your mind in early spring when
this happens. Is it a kelt? Nine times out of ten it is, but not often
on the Park Pool. I saw a small back appear in the foam as the
fish ran across, felt a surge of power and then saw the fish clearly
as it arched in the water. It was fresh! It may seem strange to
admit that I sometimes tremble for a six- or seven-pounder. I
should add that this most often happens in February. This was

the first fish of the season for me and it had been an unproductive week so far. It was well hooked, however, and after the usual display came to the net and was safely ashore. A small, shining fish, rather thin; blue and pink shone through its scales but there were no sea lice. Six pounds only, but the most welcome bag, breaking my own ice for the season.

Ice in sheets on pools is curious stuff. I first met it years ago on an early March day on the Helmsdale on beat 6 – the beat with the Kildonan falls at its head. We arrived at the Manse Pool, a slowish pool with a good lie known as the Swirlies or Swirls at its tail. The stream was open, but the main pool and the Swirlies were covered in a sheet of clear, thin ice. The ghillie, George Hardy, and I decided we would break the ice off and hope that the pool would fish in the afternoon. We started at the headstream and as we broke off the first large sheet of ice two fresh fish, most likely startled by our activities, ran up the low stream above with their backs out of the water. I thought for sure we were ruining the pool, but in for a penny in for a pound, and we set to the task of floating off the large sheets of ice by severing their connection with the stones and the grass and gently punting them out into the stream, where they floated sedately down, occasionally heaving up over stones, cracking and rearing up as the current took them away. We went right down to the Swirlies, made a magnificent job of clearing the pool, and examined our handiwork. I knew we had disturbed the water badly, but the Manse without its ice looked splendid, so I tried my fly down it. I expected nothing; after all, we had waded the pool and broken ice off and caused some disturbance. However, I had a solid good take in the Swirlies, played the fish for twenty seconds and lost it. It was incredible that a fish should come to the fly so soon after our ice breaking. Well, it was incredible then, but I know now that this is not at all uncommon. I left the lie after losing my fish, tried another corner and returned to the Swirlies. This time I was again into a fish, which did not get off and was duly landed. It was a remarkable example of breaking ice off an unfishable pool and immediately or very shortly after that getting into a fish. I was vigorously reminded of at least one nineteenth-century eccentric who had his man thoroughly stone and pole a pool on the Spey before he fished it. Now, I still do not believe that that is the way to treat a salmon pool, but I have no doubt whatever that ice broken and floated off a lie seems not only to leave it still fishable, but may in fact give the fish a sense of release and bring them on to the take.

The Helmsdale in February is not for the faint-hearted. It can be hard labour for little reward in terms of fish on the bank. Much of the spring river is gentle moorland fishing, or it would be gentle if the wind would die down. Yet I must not malign the wind. On beats like 4 and 3, where there are excellent pools cut deeply into the peat, leaving little flow, almost what they call on the Thurso 'dead water', wind and the technique of backing up can bring great sport. I like to see an upstream wind raising waves like the sea. I have seen Kilfedir, the Baddy Wood and Dalhalomy white with waves and fishing well. In gentle conditions they can be impossible to fish.

Backing up is one of the ways to fish slowish pools rippled by the wind. It is really an incredible form of fishing. You start down near the tail of the pool. By art or more likely by brute force, you put out a long line and, as you retrieve, you walk backwards slowly, taking a couple of steps up the pool before re-casting. Now, walking backwards on a level highway would be fairly easy, if ill advised. Walking backwards up the bank of a Highland river is, to some minds, consummate folly. Further, backing up needs wind, and on the Helmsdale in February you sometimes get winds with all the qualities of a hurricane. It may be snowing or raining too. The picture, then, is of a poor soul, heavily swathed in layers of waterproof, hammering out a long line and a large fly into a gale and walking backwards as he fishes. I am sometimes surprised that the men in the white coats do not suddenly emerge from the heather to take me away. I comfort myself, however, with what all madmen know. I am not only sane; I am wise. The Helmsdale has, over the years, produced far more fish for me through backing up than it has to normal downstream fly.

As a write I remember getting into four early springers one after the other at the tail of Kilfedir, on beat 2. There was also the memorable afternoon on Lower Torrish when it not only blew hard upstream but produced horizontal snow. The other rod was having a last cold cast on the headstream and the ghillie was taking shelter from the snow, having witnessed me backing up the pool at least twice to no effect. It was extremely difficult to get the fly out that day and I remember feeling cussedly satisfied every time the line straightened and the fly sailed across the broad tail of the pool. I fished the pool, handlining with cold hands, with my face getting stung as the snow beat into it. Halfway up, I had him – a sudden pull and he was on in that maelstrom of black waves with the snow still streaming over it. He was very fresh, twelve pounds in weight, the product of near-manic perseverance. But I doubt whether I would have exchanged that fish for two caught on a May morning.

Perseverance is one of the cardinal virtues of February fishing on the Helmsdale. You can fish the whole week without touching a springer, but this is offset by the sudden encounters one has with superb springers. On beat 1, in low cold water one February, I spent the morning breaking sheet ice off Salscraggie (the maps call it Solus Craggie). My companion Ian Neale, Johnnie Hardy, my excellent ghillie and companion, and I floated off what seemed like tons of ice. The beat produced nothing during the day and I was scuppered by five o'clock, having waved my rod all day, walked backwards up rocky banks in backing up, broken ice off several pools and been into only two kelts. Ian was similarly tired. At five o'clock I said weakly, 'Well, you do the bottom pools once more and I'll try Salscraggie.' We had lacked wind for much of the day and the evening looked as if it would bring its usual calm. Salscraggie needs wind, except at its head, but to fish the head well you have to ford the river and fish the right bank. I was too tired to bother, and anyway I found a breeze working its way up the open water of the pool and ruffling the narrows above. I fished the head down, rather quickly, and tried the narrows. I was very tired indeed by this time and I could feel my casting getting sloppy. Time to quit, I thought. Yet the breeze on the tail seemed to lure me back again to the broad open water above the boat and near the mouth of the small burn.

I should, perhaps, explain that this pool lies hard under the road and at one point near the tail the newly erected crash barrier is irksomely near and can cause trouble on the back cast. I was, as I say, tired. On positively my last backing up of the pool, at about twenty to six in the evening, which means dusk in February, I made my cast, heard the fly hit the crash barrier, and,

11

on checking, found it had broken off. Wouldn't that have been the time to stop? It was a favourite fly, however – a two-inch Willie Gunn. I climbed the bank, looked on the road and there, intact, lay the fly. I checked the cast, took off a frayed six inches or so and tied on the fly again to finish my backing up of the pool.

At the burn mouth, on my second cast after starting, I had a take and was into the nicest, hardest, cleanest springer I had seen for years. It forged up to the narrows, steamed down to the tail, hammered away in the stream off the burn mouth and, in a word, fought excellently. A car stopped behind me, then a van. Two men got out and stood on the crash barrier without saying a word. I was afraid they would come and offer to net out the fish, since the ghillie was downstream. I never allow strangers to net my fish, particularly hard-sought springers. I usually say, 'Well, I'm rather eccentric, you see, and I insist on netting my own.' Not true, of course. But horror stories abound of helpers emerging to net a fish, knocking it off and walking away saying 'Sorry!' My great friend Oliver Williams, fishing Dalhalomy on the Helmsdale, had precisely that experience. 'Sorry!' said the anonymous netsman, who had clearly never netted a salmon in his life, as he walked off, got into his car and went. My silent audience, standing on the crash barrier, did not offer, I'm glad to say. My fish, by now tired out, slid in over the stream at the end, lying thick and beautiful in the water, and I was able with a slight struggle to get my Gye net under him and with persuasion got him to fold into it. Thick fish can be hair-raising to net because of this. This one, however, was up the bank, on to the road, dispatched, admired and tucked into a bass in no time at all. I drove down to where Ian had finished, lower on the beat. He had scales, and weighed my fish at seventeen pounds exactly. It was an absolutely magnificent salmon, and I didn't feel tired at all. Perseverance had proved to be the Helmsdale's main February virtue.

It is a fascinating river to try early in the season, but often it can be very hard to find a fish in. Yet the two or three you might get for the week seem to be memorable above all other fish. I don't think Ian Neale will ever forget one of his February fish from beat 1. Again, it was at the end of the day. The morning had been unproductive, in a low, cold water. Just after lunch, however, Ian had taken a fine ten-pounder from the head of Salscraggie, but this had been the only sport of the day. On one of the lower pools, the Lower Caen, I had seen a fish move at lunch time, but had failed to get any response. Ian was taken down by Johnnie to fish the lower river and I was sent to try all the little corners below Salscraggie – the Stall, the excellent Alder, the Sands and the Viaduct. I had two kelts. As I emerged from the cutting at the Viaduct I saw Ian and Johnnie standing close together on the bank of the Lower Caen. Talking, I thought. I tried the Caen stream. Nothing. I looked down again, and they appeared to be still standing talking. Wasting time, I thought. I fished the Upper Caen and by this time was wondering what on earth was going on on the Lower Caen below. I could stand it no longer. I reeled in, walked down and, as I neared them, saw that Ian was playing a fish, and apparently had been all the time I was fishing. Ian looked grim and rather the worse for wear.

Johnnie said, 'We've been into this fish for an hour and by Jove he's been giving it stick!' 'Is it foul hooked?' I asked. 'I thought so at the beginning,' said Johnnie, 'but I don't think so now.' Just then a tail came out of the water.

I said very knowledgeably that I thought it was a good fish, sixteen or seventeen pounds, and that I was sure they would get it out soon. In the meantime I was going to spend the last twenty minutes of light on the Whinnie below, where there was a chance of a fish. Ian was clinging on to his rod with a very serious expression, saying his arms were killing him.

I did not see the end of that fight, and I regret it. The fish was forever getting new wind and it was only at the last minute that it showed any signs of going off balance and showing its side.

When it did so, it was clear that it was not seventeen pounds, nor anywhere near it. It would not fit into the net and Johnnie, a powerful and fit man, got into the water and tailed it, getting it ashore and up the bank in a most impressive show of strength, Ian said. I saw the fish immediately afterwards, fins still erect, and it was an astonishing salmon. It weighed twenty-eight and a half pounds, was short, very thick in the beam, a great male fish straight from the sea. It had engulfed the Willie Gunn and was hooked well back in the mouth, immovably. I have never seen a bigger springer. I believe that turned out to be the biggest salmon for over a decade from the Helmsdale and the biggest February fish ever known. I don't think it has been passed yet, but a couple of summer fish in 1982 came close.

I would not like my readers to think that the Helmsdale is prolific in February. It is not, and it is very hard work. Two of us often fish all week for two fresh fish between us and the prospect of a blank week is always there, right in front of us. Half a dozen in a prolific year would be memorable, but it rarely happens. One year, astonishingly, produced thirteen in the February week. Remarkable. But it is gripping fishing. There are some good fish available from time to time. Mostly, the fish are small, six or seven pounds, pleasing the ghillies, who say 'Small springers mean a year of plenty.' I think they are right, and I love to start the season like that. But I have now, over the seasons, seen fish from seventeen pounds up to twenty-eight with others in the mid-teens as well as the smaller springers. Helmsdale can do it and when it does taking these big fish on fly in a small river, ironically enough often in dead-low cold water, is remarkable. It is quite different from taking such fish on the bait in the Tay, or on fly in the large pools of the Dee.

The Helmsdale is a memorable, beautiful small river in exciting, unspoiled country, excellently run as a salmon fishery and managed with vision and care. I have developed a very deep affinity with the water and with its serene moorland setting. Even in its blank days, when you are fishless, cold and tired, the Helmsdale never fails somehow to give you a blink of promise. Perhaps it is that, on a small river, where you know the very stones well, a fishless day is illuminated by your memory of productive days. Rivers with pools like the sea never give this degree of intimacy.

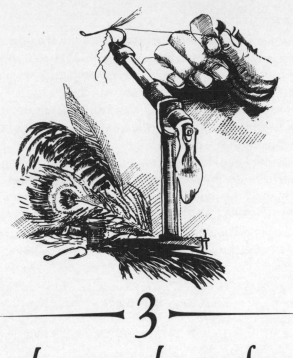

3

The Nearly Perfect Salmon Fly

The design and dressing of salmon flies is in a state of permanent evolution. It is also, within that evolution, subject to waves of fashion, to changes in technology and to what might be called the politics of the fishing world. Rules and regulations change, usually reflecting attitudes to how salmon fly-fishing should be conducted. For example, if the river authorities on the Tweed judge that abuses are taking place in the fishing of certain types of fly, the leaded tube for instance, they legislate to rectify the situation, and that change in policy is soon reflected in the kind of flies being fished, and being tied for sale on Tweedside.

We inherited a remarkable tradition of salmon flies from the Edwardian and Victorian sportsmen. I am sure we have all seen the large single-hooked flies, usually with gut loops for the eye, or, if they are earlier than that, tied directly on tapered hooks with gut links. There flies at first were local, tied to suit certain rivers. For example, look into Scrope's *Days and Nights of Salmon Fishing on the Tweed* (1843), of which I am happy to have a first edition with the etchings with their original colour. His flies were rather dowdy, tied with available natural furs and wool and feathers, including turkey, various duck feathers and hackles which could have been collected from farmyard hens on Tweedside. Let me quote Scrope's dressing for Meg in her Braws, perhaps the most elaborate of the six flies he quotes. 'Braws', by the way, means finery; the Scots word 'braw', often used as an adjective ('A braw day' or 'A braw, clean fish'), is still in use today. Used as a noun and in the plural, it is less common and might be best translated in the fly name as 'Meg in her Sunday Best'.

MEG IN HER BRAWS

Wings	Light brown, from the wing of a bittern
Head	Yellow wool
Next the Head	Mottled blue feather from a jay's wing
Body	Brown wool mixed with bullock's hair
Towards the end of the body	Green wool; next to that, crimson wool
Tail	Yellow wool
Round the body	Gold twist; over that, cock's hackle, black at the roots and red at the points

Scrope's flies were obviously very successful yet none of them exist today. He names six, and if anyone knows of any of these patterns being used today, even by an individual, it would be interesting to hear of it. The flies are Kinmont Willie, The Lady of Mertoun, Toppy, Michael Scott (which he describes as 'a most killing wizard' and graces with an Italian couplet in its praise), Meg with the Muckle Mouth (Meg wi' the Muckle Mou'), and Meg in her Braws. The names are full of references to Tweedside, especially that part of Tweed between Galashiels and Kelso. Michael Scott was the local legendary wizard of the Eildon Hills, near Melrose.

These flies were good, but they were largely supplanted on the Tweed and elsewhere by what I have sometimes called the Irish invasion. In the middle and late nineteenth century, much

16

more gaudy flies appeared on the salmon-fishing scene, tied with exotic feathers from Africa and the Far East, reflecting the opening up of the world to trade and the establishment of the Empire. What a gaudy lot they were! They had peacock, toucan, Indian crow, golden pheasant crest, jungle cock and numerous dyed feathers from a whole aviary of birds. They were fished, normally on single hooks up to 8/0 in size, and they flashed and glittered in almost every pool of every salmon river of note in Scotland. I just caught the end of this fashion. I caught my first salmon on fly in the early 1950s on a Silver Wilkinson single. I had some fine early fish on the Dusty Miller and I heard anglers all around swearing by the Silver Doctor, Jock Scott and that gaudiest of all flies, the Durham Ranger, which seemed to me to be tied with bunches of pheasant feather as if to reconstruct a golden pheasant cock strutting in his prime.

These exotic and rather expensive flies were spectacular and you could feel the pressure of fashion to have a box (or a book with felt pages) well decorated with them. But in Ayrshire, where I was brought up and caught my first salmon, there was also a continuing tradition of duller-coloured flies, such as Brown Turkey or Grey Turkey, very much more in the direct line of descent from Scrope than the exotic flies I have blamed on Ireland and the Empire. In the Highlands, also, local traditions of fly dressing existed, using local materials to good effect. Flies such as the Hairy Mary became well established, starting I am not sure when, but certainly used extensively in the early decades of this century. The Hairy Mary has a hair wing, and it was the first hair-winged fly I ever saw. It uses natural deer's hair (red deer) and, although it has innumerable variations of colour and type of hair used (most dressers think red deer's hair is too coarse and brittle), the fly is still in wide use today and I have in my box a number of Hairy Mary flies dressed for spring use and for low-water use. Indeed, I regard this fly as having a special kind of magic for rivers in the West Highlands. I use it there, in waters like the Shiel, in lightly dressed low-water doubles and I have had some memorable takes on that fly. There is something about the combination of brown hair wing (I like the darker, softer hairs) and the blue hackle with the best of all bodies, black silk ribbed with gold, which works well in the west. Now that dressing may not be the

17

original, but it is the one I am most familiar with. It shows the continuing evolution of dressings, moving towards, we all hope, the perfect salmon fly.

So far I have spoken of salmon flies dressed on conventional single hooks and on doubles, although I may have hinted that hooks may be heavy irons or light low-water irons. This is clearly a technical matter. Modern hooks can be superior in strength and design to hooks our grandfathers used. It has also to be said, however, that modern hooks, which may be mass-produced and sometimes carelessly rushed on to the market, can lack the fine hand finishes of hooks of an earlier day. Hooks must be reliable – neither too hard and brittle on the one hand, nor too soft and flexible on the other. I have gone through agonies with faulty hooks, especially faulty trebles (I now use trebles very extensively on my salmon flies – on tubes, Waddingtons and Waddington-type flies). Hooks, really, cannot be entirely machine-made. In their tempering and other processes, the eye of the craftsman is still essential. Our flies today have moved into tubes, which use trebles; Waddingtons, which use forged shanks and trebles; and wire-bodied flies (which I call Brora flies), which use trebles. The whole perspective on salmon flies has altered, partly because of the advent of the reliable eyed treble hook, but partly because we no longer think of the salmon, as an Edwardian guest at a Highland shooting lodge might, as a fish which can be tempted by gaudy colours, as a missionary in former years might have won the attention of a tribe of natives on some exotic shore by using beads and fabrics. We think far more biologically about the salmon today. We think of food formerly hunted in the sea and still present in the reflexes of the fish in the river. We know salmon were once parr, and we know they rose well to trout flies. Our flies, therefore, reflect the types of food known to the salmon in its feeding phases, which may stir a reflex feeding take. I know well that there are other types of take, and other very successful flies for certain circumstances (can one ever forget the rory General Practitioner?) but for the most part our most successful flies have settled down to tubes, Waddingtons and Brora flies, making use of colour, it is true, but also using different sorts of natural hair. Summer flies especially are sober, natural and non-assertive creations.

18

Salmon flies which please me, and which do so because they please the salmon too, have, over the years fallen more and more into one main type. I use few conventional flies for salmon, although it is interesting that I still use standard single-hook flies for sea trout, with one on pretty well every cast I make up. I am trying as I write to remember the last salmon I caught on a single-hook fly. I can remember several which fell to sea-trout flies, in river and loch. There were the very early fish, of course, caught on singles because I had little else. But I am stumped. I cannot date the last fish which took a conventional single. My low-water flies are either light doubles or are small Broras or tubes. My spring flies are Broras or Waddingtons or tubes, with the occasional large double. I carry a box of rather nicely dressed singles, but, apart from borrowing a few to fish on lochs for sea trout, I have not wet one for about five years. I may have gone too far in my movement towards treble-hooked flies and in my love of the low-water double, and it might be interesting to rediscover the delights of fishing singles, especially low-water singles, but I have to say that I find certain types of the Waddington and Brora flies so effective that I am thirled to them.

What are these nearly perfect salmon flies? Let me describe one or two in detail, but let me also say that I fish the Tweed, Helmsdale and Brora in early spring, wet a fly in the Tay in the early weeks, regularly fish the Dee in both February and May, fish Highland and Hebridean waters in summer, and enjoy the Tweed in autumn. I have to give an apologia to explain something about my fly selection. Flies are for waters and times and conditions. I dare say I would not fish these patterns regularly if I were a regular Wye fisher, or a west-coast rather than an cast-coast fisher. Equally, I fish waters where these flies are regarded as proper and respectable, and I firmly believe they are. It is not inconceivable that some beats might ban the treble, on a mistaken notion about sport. In that case my box would tell a different story.

The Brora fly owes a great deal to the theories of Richard Waddington, who popularised a theory about salmon flies in the immediate post-war years in which he held that the natural food of the salmon as it approaches our rivers is the elver. He thus proposed his Waddington Elverine lure, dressed on a forged shank with a treble mounted at the tail, as a fly which would offer a better profile in the water than conventional flies, having regard to the food the salmon best liked to hunt. Waddingtons were an eye-opener and I filled my box with them in the fifties and sixties. Then I tried tying up my own, using wire as a body rather than a specially forged mount with shank and treble. I did not do very well with my own flies, because I didn't select the wire for the bodies very well. Further, about ten years ago I discovered that Rob Wilson of Brora tied up absolutely superb wire-bodied flies, dressed with the right hair wings and the right colours of body for the fishing I took in Sutherland, and, as a kind of bonus, they fished superbly in the Tweed in the autumn.

The Brora fly – I would like to call them Brora Waddingtons but I think in doing so I would be confusing the issue, and perhaps infringing a couple of patents – is dressed on a selected stainless-steel wire body. The body can be of heavier or lighter wire and can be dressed with a single loop of wire, or a loop with its tails overlapping to give added bulk and weight to the fly. In spring, when you want a large fly which fishes down into the river, Brora flies are ideal. They swim well, they hover well, and they cast well. Above all they hook well and, in February when you might get two fish for a week, every sincere offer is important.

The materials which make up the patterns of the Brora flies are just right for spring work. Perhaps the most famous pattern of them all is the Willie Gunn. This fly, named after a head keeper of Sutherland estates, has a wing of mixed yellow, orange and black hair, over a black body ribbed with gold. It is a superb fly and has won acceptance everywhere. It has invaded the Spey and the Dee with great success and is making a name for itself on the Tweed.

The Willie Gunn, by far the most glamorous of the range, is by no means the only successful pattern. There are yellow-and-black-winged flies over the same gold-ribbed black body which are first-class. I love the black-and-orange-winged flies over the standard black body. There is a pattern named after Mr Jim Pilkington, a famous Helmsdale and Brora fisher, which has a touch of blue in it and there are all-blacks, which we might mistakenly call Stoat's Tails but for the fact that no stoat could provide enough hair for these spring flies. I suspect they are dog tails or cow tails, but who in their right mind would want to change an honoured name like Stoat?

One of the great advantages of using wire-bodied flies is that you can, with a little work, change the trebles when they get blunt or broken. The treble hook on the Brora fly is attached to the body by having the wire pass through the eye. The hook is supported by a stiffener of nylon which holds it out from the body. When my hooks need changing, I use a pair of wire-cutting pliers to cut the old treble off at its eye, removing all bits from the wire of the fly body. I then put on a small split ring and attach the new hook to it. I tie on a nylon stiffener, whipping it to the treble shank and to the end of the body of the fly and I have a fly nearly as good as new. This process slightly extends the fly length. I have tried other methods but I am not skilled enough to secure the treble neatly by them (for example by using heavy nylon and a needle knot, or the same nylon whipped to the body. I have not used adhesives. I believe Rob Wilson has had great success using nylon and a touch of Araldite. My split-ring repairs work well, and have the great advantage that I can change the hooks by the riverside, with very little work. Mind you, I prefer changing the hooks in my hotel in the evening, and leaving the day for fishing, so I carry spares.

Brora flies started with me as spring flies, and they were splendid things to fish in the Helmsdale in spring, but recently I have found the smaller versions, say one inch long, excellent in the Dee fishing in May, especially if there is high water. I had a superb fish on a small black and orange on the floating line in Dee in May 1983, a shining fish of twenty-one pounds, and I have had many less spectacular ones also. These flies swim well, which means that they assume a horizontal attitude in the water. They can be fished at different depths, but I have no knowledge of using very heavy flies hard on the bottom. I believe in fishing my flies up from the bottom, even in freezing water in spring.

Waddingtons, dressed on their own forged shanks, have a great deal to recommend them, especially their lightness. This hinders casting, but greatly assists presentation in some conditions. You can get Waddingtons dressed in Brora colours and they do offer a useful variation on the theme, providing lighter flies in the large and small sizes. I have had some fine fish on

21

Dee on small, one-inch Waddingtons. I have also, recently, found the smallest Waddington shanks first-class for sea trout flies for night fishing.

The word 'perfect' is dangerous to use and in a field such as salmon-fly design it would be presumptuous to close the book of development and say, 'We have arrived at the perfect fly.' That is why I refer to the Brora flies as nearly perfect. To make them slightly better, I would ask for a really easily detachable and replaceable treble and I would ask for a lighter and smaller version of the fly for summer floating-line fishing. I know that in Sutherland, when the water drops away and summer fish are pursued, they fish the most exquisite small doubles and small-dressed trebles of the Drury type. A separate tradition takes over there, because low-water fishing in summer means just that. On Dee and Spey and Ness, for example, low water still means lots of water and, while the Dee particularly does well with small doubles, I think there is a case for a special light Brora fly for these conditions. These improvements are rather like the exceptions which prove the rule, however. They emphasise that, for much of the year and for most of my fishing, the Brora wire-bodied flies are dangerously close to perfection.

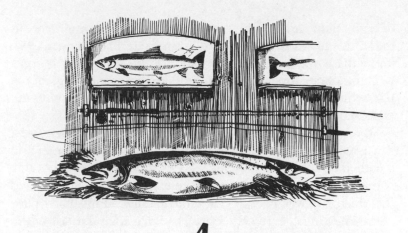

4

Three Tay Days

I suppose the Tay is not a large river in world terms. I know from my fishing in Lapland that it is only a fraction of the Tana. I know equally well that when I stood beside one of the rapids on the St Lawrence in Canada I had difficulty in equating it with any river I had ever seen or imagined. But in Scottish terms the Tay is impressively large. I have stood on the Perth bridge and have experienced a kind of angler's vertigo thinking of the endless tons of water the town stream pulls down from the North Inch flats. Equally dizzying is the notion of the millions of salmon which have run up under that bridge even during its lifetime of a century or so. The continuity of the Tay impresses too. It is, to me, a river which probably runs fish every day of every year. There is certainly a great, almost unknown, winter run; there is a well-known and much-sought-after spring run from January to May. That spring run can merge with the more spasmodic summer runs of fish, the grilse and the larger salmon and the sea trout. If there is a pause in the year it is somewhere in the summer, but by middle or late August the often spectacular autumn runs start and can build up to impressive presentations of fish right up to the rather early rod-closing date in mid-October. Closing dates are arbitrary in natural terms. We know the autumn run goes on and we suspect that it merges with the rather mysterious and little-known winter runs of big fish, which in turn merge in November and December with the earliest of the new springers heading for Loch Tay.

How can I characterise the fishing year of the Tay? The easiest way is to choose a day early in spring, a day in early summer and a late day at the beginning of October. Before I do that something has to be said about recent Tay fishing. I have fished the river for over twenty years and I must admit that I have sometimes in recent years felt that I have seen the last of the great fishing on the river. It is still a productive and memorable place to fish, but – am I right? – it has changed radically from being a river of runs of salmon to being a river of batches. I hope it is not just distance lending enchantment to the statistics, but in the mid-sixties, when I used to get the odd day on Redgorton, I can remember years when the spring run by the end of April had produced four hundred fish. And were the September days of fifteen fish, and better, on Almondmouth unusual? There used to be real point in taking the boats off in early May on the Tay and declaring, officially, that the spring fishings were largely over, because, although fish still ran in numbers and excellent fishing could be had with the continuing runs or the batches of late springers, the estates regarded early May as the end of the fishing of spring quality.

I must put my cards on the table when I talk about the Tay. I was never the regular tenant of a great, named beat. I did get regular single days on these waters, sometimes as a guest and sometimes as a paying guest. I had my regular day-a-fortnight fishing for some years at Burnbane, just below Caputh. I fished Stenton on a multiple-day basis for some years, mainly in the seventies, and I took days up and days down river as they came. So in my twenty-odd years on this river I have sampled it quite widely and have tried it through the season. It was a generous river to me, but not embarrassingly so.

Perhaps I was not a typical Tay angler and this made me see the river through other lenses. For instance, I have never really settled for harling – fishing from a boat which trails, hangs and swings the bait (and sometimes the fly) over the stream below.

24

Some of the beats I liked best had no boats anyway. I just couldn't settle to sitting in the back of a Tay boat with one of the rods out of the back technically belonging to me, as, with the others, it harled a Devon, or a Toby or a Kynoch Killer over the lies. Every so often a rod would bow as a fish took and, if it was yours, you lifted it, were into him, and possibly found yourself playing a salmon which I never felt I had fished for and certainly never felt I had hooked.

As my acquaintance with the Tay grew, I found myself questioning the pleasures of harling, wondering whether day-long bank spinning was not sometimes a bit mindless and wondering whether I would not be better off fly-fishing the Tay, with occasional spinning, much as I would fish the Spey. So the Tay and I struck up a relationship where I offered to treat it differently, to fish it with fly, wading it as I would the Spey or Dee, and in return all I asked for was a certain amount of encouragement, a fish or two here and a fish or two there. Tay ghillies thought I was touched and in the memorable direct way they often have of expressing themselves they told me so. I asked my guests at Burnbane, for instance, no matter the time of year, to try the fly for a couple of hours at least during the day. There were some interesting eye-openers. We had the first springer of the year on fly on more than one occasion. Sometimes we would fish our way through our January days with alternate fish on fly and Devon or Toby. In summer, fly outshone any spun bait, especially in the low water. In autumn, fly could do extremely well and I and my colleagues had some marvellous sport – days of bent rods and pulsing fish.

What I used to advocate in spring was to fish fly on a slow-sinking line, concentrating on the 'scallops' of water which the streams bit out of the shingle beside the main streams. Burnbane had some splendid lies in gravel like this. The lies were not only washed out of the shingle laterally, showing in little bays on the bank, but were dug out of the shingle bed of the stream. It was ideal fly water. I liked two-inch Brora Waddingtons or similar flies, with yellow and black hair in their tying. I wrote about this and the fun my colleagues and I were having in rediscovering the Tay as a fly-fishing river and in 1968 I received a charming and encouraging letter from an experienced Tay angler who was called, I think, Hay. I only have the first page of that letter still in my possession but I think it ought to be quoted in full because it so clearly states the case for early Tay fly-fishing.

Braehead, Hatton Road,
Kinnoul, Perth
7 April 1968

Dear Mr Currie

Your notes on fly fishing in the early months on a beat which I think I recognise (Burnbane – or more properly the old name Burnbrae?) struck a responsive chord in one who also takes his fly rod out in the early weeks.

There are times and places where the fly will beat the spinner – especially in January in *high* water. On most beats there is usually a little pocket at the near side of a stream where running fish will rest. On the 1st February 1967 I took five fish from such a pocket when the boat got only one from the only pool it could fish on Taymount.

I use the heaviest quick-sink line on a Sharpe's 15 ft spliced cane rod. Cast square across on a slack line. When it comes into really slack water retrieve by hand very slowly – fish usually take firmly on the second pull. Ordinary flies – even doubles and Waddingtons, were not effective so I evolved my own. Since the line goes right down, weight in the fly is unnecessary. The lure must have life and offer no resistance when the fish gulps it. And it must be at least four inches long and offer no leverage.

At this point Mr Hay went on to give instructions on making up his large, light spring flies. He took a length of 24 lb nylon and, laying it round the joint of a tapered treble hook, he spliced it firmly on. He firmly whipped the heavy nylon to form the basis of the fly body and on to this he dubbed a black wool body, added gold tinsel, and at the head and tail of this long fly he added hot-orange hackles. The fly finished up looking like a fore-and-aft creation, with orange fins and orange tail and gold-ribbed black between. These flies he tied up in huge sizes, four and even five inches. But they were light and as he went on to say in his letter,

From the rear in the water it looks like a poised minnow and the fish gulp it right back so that I usually have to extract it from the gill covers. It does not work after February or in smaller sizes. I have used it up to five inches when I incorporate a second treble halfway up the body. The rear hackle is the more important. Wings are no use, nor hackles along the body. In other words it is a minnow or fry to the fish and the hackles are the tail and fins.

I treasure this fragment of a letter from a thoughtful and experienced angler. His approach is slightly different from mine. I do find smaller flies working well and I find that they work right through the spring, and it may be that my friend's insistence that the flies do not work after February relates to the sizes he prefers. Equally, I think he is teaching us a very important lesson about salmon fly size in spring. It was Waddington who noted that a salmon more often prefers a fly of above three inches to a fly smaller in size. He was, of course, propounding the elverine theory. I wonder whether Mr Hay of Perth was in fact doing the same thing. His black four-inch, flexible, light creations with gills or fins and tails cannot be far off a slightly souped up elver. His excellent description of fishing a slack line to gain depth and handlining slowly through the sheltered lies beside the stream is classical. He is not merely spinning with a fly rod, as some would accuse. He is doing several things with fly which the spinner could not replicate with bait. He is presenting a light, swimming bait of some size which fishes up from the shingle, and he is fishing a slow bait which does not seek bottom but moves with every variation of the stream.

Ghillies and other anglers, seeing me fish in January and February with a large, long fly and with a long rod and sinking line, sometimes say, 'Why fly-fish with tackle like that? You might as well be spinning.' This seems to me to be standing the available facts on their head. Shouldn't it be 'Why spin, if you can catch them on fly by fishing like this?' It in no way diminishes my pleasure as a fly-fisher to think that the salmon gulps my fly (I am indebted to Mr Hay for that evocative verb) imagining it to be a fish. No one in his right mind would look into a salmon fly box, spring, summer or autumn, and seriously suggest that its contents were in some way imitations of flies. A salmon in high water in spring or autumn and in cold water at any time of the

27

year has probably still a feeding reaction which relates to the cold waters of the North Atlantic. What flies live there? The larger end of the feeding available is probably herring or sand-eels or other fish and the smaller end of the menu is likely to be crustacea, and those marvellously colourful creatures of the plankton which the late Arthur Ransome drew our attention to in his book *Mainly about Fishing*. And do you remember Arthur Ransome's infallible fly – the Vulturine Guineafowl lure? How long was it? Mine is at least a couple of inches. And how long is a Collie Dog (if I might ask a Sellars and Yeatman-type question ranking with 'How long is a piece of string?')? The hair of a collie dog can be three or four inches, trailing far behind the treble hook on the tube, yet killing springers all over Scotland. I also recall Brook's Sunburst fly, tied for Norwegian waters. It is a three-inch black hair fly with a few gold hairs underneath. It is as light as you could tie and it fishes well in the cold rushing waters of the Laerdal.

So I fly-fish the Tay and am judged to be soft in the head as a result. Or I am seen to be fly-fishing the Tay in February with a biggish fly and am asked why I don't spin or am accused of just spinning with a fly rod. I used to fish light wooden Devons with spiral Jardine leads well up the trace and I said to my friends that I was doing this so that the minnow might fish like a fly. We are trapped in a world of definition if we believe too firmly in prescriptive labels. I see definition differently, however. The salmon has never revealed to anyone why it takes a fly or a bait. I don't much mind why. Fly-fishing, for me, is fishing fly tackle and I just love it. Fishing a big fly or a medium fly with this or that sinking line alters what my tackle does for me, but I am still fly-fishing with a fly rod and a fly line. I do not feel that my enthusiasm for fly-fishing is in any way exclusive. It is rather the reverse. My fly-fishing embraces whatever my spinning colleagues do with Devons or Wagtails or Tobies. I am not even averse to the argument that my hot-orange and black flies are shrimps or squids or minnows. If I am soft in the head because I think this way, I take comfort from the notion that I am pleasing myself and taking fish, and in recent years I have actually come to pity anglers who have the spinning twitch and who cannot settle to the pleasures of the fly rod. The Tay has taught me a great deal in this line.

Catching the first fish of the year on fly is a marvellous experience, but to catch the third on the fly and more or less to go on with fish alternately on fly and Devon, when the exposure of the fly was less than that of the bait, was an important experience for me and for some of my friends who accepted the notion that part of every day should be devoted to the fly, regardless of conditions. I shall never forget the triumph of Paul Young taking a good January springer from the shingly run – or rather from the side of it – which runs down into Burnbane pool. The gauge was at 4 feet 6 inches although the Tay was running clear. That fish fell to fly, despite our efforts all morning with Tobies and Devons. Equally memorable was Ken Evans's 15½-pounder, the third fish of the same season, taken from the same run on a long mustard and black hair tube fly his son had tied up. He was using a No. 11 Wet Cel line and fishing in a manner not unlike that described by Mr Hay earlier in this chapter. On that occasion the gauge was at 2 feet 6 inches with the river running clear. The key to this success was, I think, in the kind of lies we had to cover there. They were shallow, from two to four feet deep. The rush of the main stream kept the fresh fish holding to the side. I am sure these were fish pausing as they ran up through Burnbane. We took fish from these lies in January and February and I am sure we only failed in March because trout fishers began to appear and they waded down this margin trotting worms as soon as the season started for them. No amount of pleading and remonstration prevented this. They waded through some of the most interesting salmon lies we had, mistakenly believing that salmon fishers always wanted to fish long casts out into the deeps. True, they deferred to the salmon fishers by letting them pass down the water, but they got in again after the salmon fisher had passed and, in my view, frightened salmon from the lies as they did so.

I do not mean to start a war by this observation. It would be a war with part of my own fishing self anyway, for I am a keen trout fisher. What interested me then was that there were miles of the Tay full of trout without salmon lies, and a precious extent of river with salmon lies in shallow water. Had we been ourselves issuing the trout permits we would have specifically directed the anglers to good trout water which did not interfere with salmon fishing. Did I say 'issuing the permits'? I am certain none of the Burnbane trout fishers had permits. They just materialised and fished. The Tay was, and to some extent still is, in a state of anarchy as far as its once excellent trout fishing is concerned. There is a glimmer of hope that under a Protection Order salmon and trout interests might coexist happily again. An important part of this prospect is that, as on the Tweed, protection could lead to restocking with trout and the whole sporting scene would revive. There is too much public pressure to fish the Tay for trout to allow it to remain in a state of anarchy. Access with responsible control, followed by proper restocking and management, will satisfy everybody. An open river can become a dead river. Who wants that? Everybody's fishing rapidly becomes nobody's fishing. In my view the Tay has very nearly been ruined as a trout water of some note because no adequate regulatory framework has existed since the demise of the estates with their exclusive control and since the rise in fishing pressure has brought hundreds every weekend to fish the river. We suffered much at Burnbane in spring when anything from ten to forty trout anglers 'shared' our beat every Saturday.

In May, the Tay is an excellent fly-fishing prospect. I have a vivid picture of two days in succeeding Mays on the Meetings Pool at Murthly Castle. There the Tay divides to flow round a well consolidated and well treed island. Fishing from the right bank, we had a fine stony stream flowing down to dig a deep eddy in the main Meetings Pool just in front of the hut. The larger stream flowed between the island and the left bank and in the island stream, which is on Upper Murthly, there were some splendid lies for the fly. We had permission to fish it on some of our days and it was always very important to discover whether the smaller island stream on our side could be waded so that we might try the better lies over on the far side.

I arrived late one nice May day. I mean, I arrived at about half past nine to discover that the three other rods on the beat had been working hard at the water since breakfast time, and, as in the parable, had caught nothing. They had judged spinning to be the best method, and who is to say they were wrong? I had certainly brought my spinning rod, but, as usual, I left it in the car and decided to use it only as a last resort, or to cover water inaccessible to wading and fly. To my relief, I found the near-side stream wadable and with the help of a staff I got to the island and marched quickly up to the head of the lovely island stream. I was fishing a floating line, but I attached a Brora fly of an inch and a half in length, an orange and black, and as I neared the end of the stream, just where it picks up speed again under a tree on the left bank, I saw a fish move. It was a productive, clean move in which the salmon popped up its nose and showed a bit of back, in one excited show. I took it to be a clean, newly arrived fish.

I was just too far downstream to cover it well, so I waded out, hurried back upstream about ten yards, got in and lengthened line. I covered the spot, and got no response. Disappointing. But as I neared the end of the stream again, I saw a second fish – or was it the same one, slightly lower down? Round came the fly and it happened. The line stopped and the softest of pulls followed. I raised the rod and there he was, pulsing away in the stream, then upstream in a run, then round and down to his lie again. It was a grand fish and he was behaving well. If the fish had panicked and had run down into the deep Meetings Pool below, as summer fish have done with me there, I would have had serious difficulty with him, but this fish held his lie in the fast water, and when he ran, ran upstream into deeper cover. My colleague Ian Calcott was by now beside me on the bank, carrying his fly rod too. I think his advice was 'Great stuff! For God's sake don't lose it!' Neither of us need have worried. The Brora fly was well in and in due course Ian netted the fish for me, a splendid Tay springer, high in the shoulder and brilliant silver on the flanks. There were twenty-eight sea lice on the fish, including several with long tails – a sure sign of freshness. The fish weighed twelve and a half pounds – an excellent trophy. All the pastoral poets had said about May mornings was true. Leaves became greener as I looked, the Tay chuckled at me, summer promised to arrive on time and all seemed to be well in the best

31

of all possible worlds. It would have taken a lot to disillusion me then.

In my enthusiasm for fly fishing, I possibly convey the impression that I have never really enjoyed spinning. This is absolutely not so, and equally untrue would be any notion that I will not spin again and enjoy it thoroughly. The Tay, again at Caputh, produced one excellent day in which the wooden Devon was the bait of the day. It was the second last Saturday of the season, in early October, and we found a clear but very high river running at 6 feet 6 inches on the gauge. At that height pools change their tune. I mean that. They sound different. They also look very different and produce fishing lies which are different in every way from those you have come to identify in lower and more normal heights of water. For example, at six and a half feet, you cannot get near half the bits of bank you like casting your fly or bait from. You can wade, of course, but it is usually wading down what normally are bankside paths. Shingly cuts into the bank, where we used to sit in summer and eat lunch, are now lies, and the main streams are unapproachable torrents.

We waded down the paths and over the shingle island with its whins standing in the water and gained a high bit of shingle where we found a splendid eddy lying well back from the stream. The water was cutting into a sandy bank and curling nicely out of the eddy back into the main river. We took turns to spin our 2½-inch Devons through this lie and in a very short space of time we took four salmon, two each. After what had not been a very rewarding summer on Tay we sat back and decided we were having, or had had, a great morning and that to celebrate we would behave like gentlemen and go into Bankfoot for lunch. What possessed us, Ian Calcott and me, to leave a river as productive as that? I think we must have become a little disoriented by the success of taking four fish. There was also the problem that, in a river as big as the Tay was that day, there were few lies we could fish and we had been through the hot lie many times already. So we lunched and felt good.

We returned to the Tay about two in the afternoon and it seemed to have fallen slightly. At least, the sides of the main streams now appeared to be fishable and we had more water to cover than the productive backwater which had given us our first four fish. We each took fish from the stream and the total mounted. We decided to return all dark hens and several good fish were slipped back into the river, but were counted as sport for the day. Fish kept coming that afternoon in October and we finally packed up, having taken seventeen fish between us for the day. We took home three or four fish each, some quite fresh and one or two large cock salmon for smoking. It was an encounter with the Tay in a generous mood, the sort of thing which does not happen to order. What a river it is when it all happens!

I have neglected the Tay recently, partly because I have had access to some other exciting waters up north, but thinking about it makes me want to try it again. I think I would like to spend some summer days on the river, in the middle reaches, down from Islamouth. I'd like to wade it and try the fly on runs and glides and the tails of pools, especially when the summer batches are running. The Tay owes me little, and has given me a great deal of fishing over the years I have known it. I never became a dedicated Tay addict, however, and I doubt whether I will be hooked now on heavy spinning, harling and prawning. I'm just the wrong angler for it. But in many ways the Tay is a most exciting prospect, not least in its size, in its unpredictability and, above all, in its generosity.

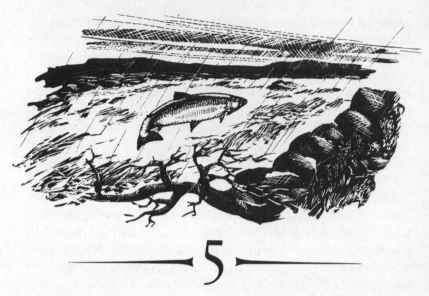

5

Salmon in High Water

There are great uncertainties in salmon fishing and they are never far from the conversation of any salmon fisher. You know the topics well. Will the spring run improve? Will the disease prove to be finally on the decline? Are grilse coming back to replace heavier fish? These and a thousand similar topics are perennial. Among them, however, lies a subject which, to my mind, is not so much an uncertainty as an anxiety. I refer to height of water. My own salmon fishing seems to be keyed into anxieties about water height far more than into disease, freshness, fish size and similar topics. I don't know whether my sign of the zodiac distorts things or not, but I am plagued by drought conditions on the one hand and excessive floods on the other. Occasionally things come right – such as on St Andrew's day in 1982, which I have written about at length in the last chapter of this book – but far more often I seem to get my fish by triumphing over the prevailing water conditions in some way.

Salmon can fish very well indeed in high water, provided the

34

colour is not too bad and subject to certain conditions of water chemistry, such as excessive acidity from peat. To illustrate this, let me describe two contrasting experiences with high water. The first of these happened early in February 1984, a few days before I wrote this chapter. I was lucky enough to be invited by a friend to join him on Upper Floors, possibly the most attractive beat on the Tweed and a wonderful place for springers on the fly. That kind of invitation is important enough to keep me awake at night, despite forty years of salmon fishing. In 1984 we had a series of heavy snowstorms in late January and early February and the rods on the Tweed managed by the skin of their teeth to get in one fishable day, the opening day, 1 February, and fish were taken over the whole length of middle and lower Tweed. So the fish were there and they were apparently in reasonable quantity. The thaw began late on 1 February and obliterated the fishings for the rest of the first week. I lost lots of sleep worrying about the possible state of the river over the weekend. I went specially to look at the middle Tweed on the Sunday, peering over Innerleithen bridge and trying to gauge the clarity of the water and whether it was rising or falling. I drove up to see the Ettrick and the Yarrow and during the day I had the misery of seeing them rise, full of snow melt-water – 'snaw bree' – on Sunday afternoon. I had something of a leaden heart on Monday, when I got a phone call to say that the river was six and a half feet up and badly coloured at Floors. Fishing was absolutely out, but I decided to go and look at the beat with this impressive flood running and, naturally, while I was there I fished a large Waddington, a three-incher, yellow and black in colour, and I confined myself to hanging it in the pockets of shelter under the bank. The water was full of sticks and straw and debris and it was absolutely unfishable.

The following night we had a sudden clearance of cloud and a sharp severe frost. Like a miracle, the Tweed fell two feet and partly cleared. Frost is an astonishing reducer of floods. It not only stops the snow melt in the hills, but it seals up every little ooze on the bank; every dependent drop of water on every blade of grass freezes; casual water in multitudes of fields becomes casual ice-covered pools. Tweed was still massively high at four feet six and was still too coloured to fish in the morning, but the telephone call told me that it might be fishable after two o'clock. I was there at ten to two, rod up, two-inch brass tube attached, with prominent black, orange and yellow hair, ready to go.

I was a little disappointed to be sent to the bottom of the beat to the New Stream, but that was the way it came out of the hat. New Stream is at the bottom of the Upper Floors water, below the turbulent, fast Slap. The left bank of the river has been heavily reinforced with a concrete wall and this deflects the stream out from the bank to form below an area of gentle water in which a boat is tethered. When I saw the sheltered bay in which the boat sat, any disappointment I had harboured at being sent there disappeared. A section of that bay was eminently fishable – perhaps ten yards, perhaps fifteen. I could get the fly out reasonably far into the stream, let the medium-sink line take it down, and then allow the fly to stop in the stream and sidle out of it into the sheltered water behind the anchored boat. If I were a salmon in a cold February flood, I thought anthropomorphically, I would lie there. I thought I felt the air warm up a degree or so as I began to fish, and my optimism soared. After two casts or so down behind the boat I had not a pull or a pluck but a tweak. Up went the rod and there he was, a springer, not a big fish but showing a very clean flank. The fish seemed to be afraid of the heavy stream and confined itself to the sheltered bay and came to the bank quite easily, as if tired out. I tailed it out, delighted to have opened my scoring for the season despite such bad conditions.

Where there is one springer, there is usually another. If that is not a proverb, it ought to be. I have had many examples of taking one fish and immediately hooking another from the same lie. In this case on the Tweed, the second fish took a yard or so further down and, quite unlike the first salmon, tore off line and forged out into the stream just after being hooked. The Tweed helped it and I had all sorts of line screaming out in the fight. I thought for one moment that this might be that exceptional thing, a large Tweed springer – rarer than radium – but the fish showed in the turmoil and it was not large at all. It was amazingly vigorous and took longer than it ought to have to come to the net. Once ashore, I laid it beside the other. Both fish were seven pounds, one slightly over and one slightly under. It

36

seemed to me that both were very lucky fish, from my point of view, being taken from a very small fishable bay in an otherwise impossible river.

I had a 3½-foot flood one March while I was fishing the Helmsdale and the way the water and the fish behaved was in sharp contrast to the Tweed. Helmsdale is a river which flows over a short course from peaty lochs and even at its clearest is as brown as sherry. When a flood comes it colours up, but tends not to go yellow, for the simple reason that yellow floods imply arable land and Helmsdale has none. That river goes turgid, then flows dirty with bits of heather and rushes and grass in it. While it may look fishable to the untutored eye, it is absolutely not so. Your fly catches on every bit of debris in the river and fishing is at a virtual standstill. Then, quite suddenly, the debris disappears as the river falls, and the river runs very black but clearing. In my case the second day was one of frustrating debris all morning, and black water all afternoon. The third day brought a black but clearing and swiftly dropping water and I began to fish with some hope. The flood had overtaken me on beat 3, while I was actually on the Lower Torrish, coming down with the speed of a greyhound and rising visibly. Beat two, one of my favourites, was lost to debris and acid, black water. The following day, beat 1 produced conditions which promised well in the morning, but took until lunch time to settle. I was by this time down on the Lower Caen Pool near the bottom of the beat. I had seen and touched nothing all morning, but when I was twenty yards above the fence which marks the lowest lie of the pool I saw a small clean fish showing. I fished my Willie Gunn over it, and watched the line coming round. It stopped, either on the rock which marks the lie there, I thought, or in a fish. I paused and raised the rod and was into a fish, which fought well and was duly netted. That fish marked the end of the bad water of the flood and it opened the scoring for a nice bit of sport on the remaining days of the week.

Waters which rise and colour up – either with silt, as in Lowland rivers, or with peat, as in Highland rivers in many areas – need time to recover from the infusion of colour. The worst rivers for colour are those waters in well farmed places. The Nith and the

Ayrshire rivers go as muddy as milky cocoa and may take a week to recover. The Tweed is not so bad, but the Ettrick can bring in bad yellowish-brown floodwater. The Leader can bring a very red flood into the river from the vale whose fields lie coloured like the *terra rossa* lands of Provence. But the Tweed fishes well with half-colour and falling water. The river which rises clear and fishes all the time, except perhaps for the period of the actual rise, is the Dee. In 1983 we had the wettest spring on record for over forty years and the Dee ran high for week after week, right through April and May. I found my May week showing anything from 4 feet 8 inches on the gauge to 'low' levels of three feet. But it was clear all the time. We caught fish in settled periods of that long flood and, while our total catch for the week was low, it was by no means a disaster. Interestingly, the fish were both in their usual places in the streams, when we could fish them, and in shelter. I suspect that the runners were in shelter and the residents were in their usual streamy lies. The limiting factor was whether we could reach the lies with the fly, since wading was very difficult, and, having reached them, whether we could fish them. There is, as experienced anglers know, a great difference between reaching a lie and fishing it. I did manage quite well at times that week and I describe in Chapter 7 a specific incident on the flooded Dee that year.

The most spectacular arrival of a natural flood I have ever seen was during the only two days I have ever fished that amazing beat on the Findhorn at Logie where gorge walls tower over deep pools and some of the stands one takes up to fish are fifty feet above the pool surface. When Ian Calcott and I arrived to fish, we were urged to get our rods up very quickly since there had been heavy rain in the hills and a flood was expected. We managed a pool each, and to fish mine I had to perch precariously on top of a cliff and cast my fly from a great pulpit-like stand. But the water had already coloured at the edges. We persevered for twenty minutes or so, wondering if we would hit one of these curious taking sprees which can mark the beginning of a rise of water, but I think we were already too late.

We went upstream of the gorge to try a long sandy pool and as we fished the water surged down, rising suddenly to alter the pools immediately. We marked the level with a stick, fished a few casts, looked back and saw the stick up to its waist in water, fished a few more casts and saw the stick floating away. The water rose two feet in fifteen minutes, bringing colour and debris and, to us, despondency. While it fell quickly the following day, our last, it did so to produce a very black peat water in which nothing looked at our flies. Spate regimes are awkward for the salmon fisher. I know rivers in the West Highlands and in the Hebrides where you set out to fish as soon as the river rises and, before your day is done, the river has fallen almost to its former level. Spates come and go and quickly rise often means quickly fall. These are, of course, natural spates and they are often very productive. Too fast a rise and too fast a fall are not good at all for fishing, however. In some areas, because of forestry drainage, very rapid rises and falls of very acid water are becoming typical and fishing is suffering. This is a serious problem throughout the Highlands and in many places in the southern hills as well. It is coupled with rainfall becoming more acidic also. Adding acid rain and fast forestry spates together we have hopeless conditions for salmon fishing and the worse environment for parr to grow in.

Possibly the worst floods of all, however, are the sudden, artificial ones which can be produced by hydro generating stations. The Tay has been dogged by daily floods of this kind for years. In certain heights of the river, the fish which have settled during the night can be unsettled by the six-inch rise in water Faskally hydro station can produce and can go off the take completely. All too often you find a fishable and productive river at eight in the morning and by nine thirty you find it has risen to produce running fish and poor sport. On some of the smaller rivers such as the Lochy sudden hydro spates can be dangerous in the extreme. Anyone who knows the Loy Mouth Pool on beat 2 of the Lochy knows that it is fished by wading down a ridge ten yards out into the stream from the left bank. It is a bad enough wade in normal, steady water, but when a sudden flood comes down from the hydro scheme above it can be dangerous. I had one bad experience there in high water. I crossed to the large island by an easy route at the end of the Bull Run and fished the Loy Mouth, but, oddly, I found fish disturbed and very uncooperative. I should have twigged what was happening that evening. It was only when I tried to get back to the island that I realised that the river was rising fast. Curiously enough, I thought at first that I was just getting tired or unfit and that at that height Loy was beginning to get the better of me. But I got to the island safely and shortly afterwards walked back to its upstream end to cross the easy neck where I had come over. Halfway across, in the dusk, I thought I must have chosen the wrong path. Had it not been easy, thigh-deep water before? I had little time for a second thought about it, because my feet were swept from me and I was turned over and swept down the back stream behind the island. It is not very dangerous there. I managed to get a grip on some bushes and I scrambled out, waders full of cold Lochy water, but with my tackle safe. I squelched up to the top of the beat where my car was parked and looked at the gauge. The river had risen eighteen inches since I started, in a ruinous flood released by the hydro dam above. I was, as they say, not too cheery about that. It had robbed me of fish, but, I reflected, had I been any longer in the Loy Mouth Pool I might have had a worse experience.

It would seem to me that natural spates, lingering on as high clearing water, are marvellous for salmon fishing, but we see fewer and fewer such rises today. Drainage is now so efficient that the sponge-like character of the land by the river is reduced. Where water flow holds, say backed by melting snow on the hills, prolonged floods, slowly falling and clearing, do result. Then high water is a great boon and fish might well come in good numbers. In these floods, salmon like consistency and rapid rises and falls of water level only serve to unsettle them. So to the anxieties of water height are added the anxieties of consistency. Without it height alone might be just another frustration.

6
The Pursuit of Depth

In a sense, all salmon fly-fishing, with the exception of two very small techniques, is concerned with depth. We sink all our salmon flies; even greased-line, or floating-line fishing as I should call it, fishes the fly sunk, albeit minimally. Midwater fly-fishing – that is, the fishing we do with slow-sinking lines – is clearly an art of the sunk fly and the cold-water fishing we do in spring and autumn is, *par excellence*, the art of sinking the fly. The exceptions are the little-tried technique of fishing dry fly for salmon – an art which I have resorted to on several occasions and have never had a fish by – and the more widely used art of dapping for salmon, which is a wider sector of fly-fishing and accounts for a respectable number of salmon in Hebridean and West Highland lochs each summer.

Getting the fly down in spring fishing, and in the conditions we meet on the Tweed from October to the end of November, is really an art of sinking the line – or so it seems to me. I have an antipathy towards leaded flies which dredge the bottom of pools. Indeed, I regard dredging heavy flies as little more than

41

sniggling as it is practised on some ticket waters on Tweed in autumn. That form of fly-fishing, with its extraordinary terminal tackle of a large heavy brass tube, sometimes tied with lead in the body or weighted by lead wire, pierced bullets, lead heads or other weights on the fly and assisted by large sea swivels on the leader, is no part of fly-fishing at all. The 'fly' itself is often an extraordinary creation, in its worst examples being an undisguised sniggling treble, on middle Tweed sometimes nicknamed a 'Walkerburn Angel'. I have nothing to say about this art, except to condemn it, and declare that it is no part of sunk-line fly-fishing whatever and is a disgrace and a shame to the club waters (and elsewhere) where it is practised.

However, I cannot resist recalling a very amusing tale. A friend of mine, an expert fishing photographer, was on the Tweed at Walkerburn and found himself shoulder to shoulder with a chap fishing the Walkerburn Angel, obviously raking the pool. You know the style, I'm sure. The line and fly are cast a little upstream and mended to allow the heavy line (often a lead-core or a fast-sinking head) to sink with its trace with swivels and its sniggling lure masquerading as a fly on the end. The water washes the line round, bumping it over stones and swinging the lure lethally round over the lies. When the line stops the sniggler heaves up his rod, intending to foul hook the salmon – if it is a salmon – which he has encountered. The lure inflicts grievous bodily harm; what it does not hold it scores or tears. Well, my friend was there and the sniggler got into a fish. Out came the camera and pictures were taken, with the fellow remonstrating and cursing the photographer. He, clearly, assumed he had sniggled the fish and so did everybody else there. The fish came ashore and, surprise, surprise, was hooked in the mouth, quite properly. That misguided Tweed salmon had actually taken the sniggler's 'Angel'. It was, as they say, a real hoot of a situation. Quite untypical.

I am a keen fisher of the slow-sinking or ordinary sinking line. I do not like fast-sink lines and I find fast-sinking heads very awkward to cast and fish well. I believe that such fast-sinking lines are not necessary in the majority of fly-fishing situations. Indeed, I will go further; I do not think they fish the fly well. They find the bottom too quickly and, on most rivers with rocky and shingly bottoms, this means that the fly is jigged and halted and jerked as it comes round. In my experience, this is poor fly-fishing. We want the fly to fish up from the bottom, even if deep. We want the fly to swim, to come round with the stream, to hover over lies and flutter in the current. We want the fly to be part of the whole stream environment, not as jetsam, but as a credible swimming creature. Heavy flies are dead, except in the fastest water. I dare say it is possible to give them some life by handlining them, but it is really rather daft to rob the fly of life by over-weighting it and then go to some trouble to restore a semblance of life to it again. It reminds me of the eighteenth-century landscape gardeners who removed all traces of rude nature from their land and then spent lots of time and money in restoring wild copses and waterfalls, by art rather than by nature.

Salmon do not lie deep, unless they are disturbed. The most productive salmon lies are four or five feet deep. One reason for the Dee being such a prominent salmon river is that it is a shallow stream. I am often stunned to see water like, say, Lower Invercauld, where you feel you can see every stone on the bottom, yet find that the beat is hotching with salmon which you did not suspect. You can wade over salmon all too easily in the Dee. I know there are exceptions where we can peer down from a bridge and see salmon lying in the deeper water of the bridge pool below. I know they appear there, but I do not expect to fish them there, nor to take fish from these deep holes. When we talk about getting the fly down to salmon in spring we are referring to putting the fly two or three feet down only.

Getting the spring fly down by this amount may seem to many to be a modest task, but I find that it can take a lot of skill to do it properly in many circumstances. Broadly, we get the fly down by using a sinking line. My favourite is a Wet Cel DT–10–S. This is what I call an ordinary sinking line, not a super sink or a high-density line and, above all, not a weighted line, the worst of which have lead cores. The lines I like settle fairly slowly into the river and they reach their fishing depth without pulling down into the water. To achieve the right depth of fly, you really need to fish the right length of line. My No. 10 Wet Cel II seems to me to fish best in spring and autumn when I have from twenty to twenty-five yards out. This has two advantages. The line sinks best where it is heaviest because it is the dressing which makes it sink, and the dressing is thickest on the belly of the line and not on the taper. The second advantage of having a longish line out is that you have mending capacity. Simply, this means that you have enough line to roll a loop upstream as soon as you cast and let the line go down for the first yard or so rather slackly, sinking with the current. As soon as you tighten and begin to fish the fly round, the action of the rod stops a good part of the sinking action. You will notice that the line really only sinks effectively when it comes round below you – when it gets into a small angle with the stream, offering least stream resistance. At a zero angle, when the line is in neutral, as it were, with regard to the stream, you have maximum sinking effect.

There are exceptions to this, but they should be seen as atypical. In deep sandy pools, such as dams or peat holes, sea trout will sometimes show a preference for a fly on the bottom, or very close to it. I have, on occasion, called this ledgering a fly for sea trout. It may be that roving sea trout disturb the deep, inert fly and make it work, as food might be disturbed by a big fish roving through a pool.

Some of the deepest flies I fish are from boats on the Tweed. It is possible for the line to get into a neutral angle behind the boat and achieve maximum depth and be handlined over the lies there. The fly can sometimes be effectively fished by the boat itself, almost in a harling style, but handlining is better fishing. On the deepest section of the Boat Pool at Bemersyde, the rod in the boat can be successful fishing in this way. I have certainly hooked fish there which were very far down indeed, say ten feet below the surface. But there, again, catching fish as deeply as that is not typical of the pool. Its shallower headstream fishes very productively and its fine middle and tail lies fish well, from the right bank particularly, in water five or six feet deep.

We do well to remember that the salmon is a shallow-swimming and shallow-feeding fish. The bag nets set their leaders down to six feet from the surface and salmon are effectively guided in to the nets by them. Sea drift nets are of shallow draught. In my opinion, salmon in really deep lies are there for some particular reason, perhaps fear or the need for shade. Occasionally kelts and spring salmon will be found in deep lies because they are out of the rush of the stream. Fresh fish do not stay in such lies long, however. They tail back into shallower water or they move up into streamy lies if they are undisturbed, or if they do not feel vulnerable.

It is interesting to reflect that five months of the salmon-fishing season are likely to be sunk-lure months – January (where rivers are open), February, March, October and November (if open). April can be a half-and-half month. This leaves May, June, July, August and September as floating-line months – another five months. The salmon fly-fisher who takes some spring and some autumn fishing, and who takes floating-line fishings in spring and summer where he can, is thus likely to be fully equipped for sunk-line and fully equipped for floating-line fishing. I do it by carrying two reels for my fifteen-foot carbon 'Yorkshire' fly rod. One reel has an AFTM 10 floating line on it and the other carries an AFTM 10 sinker. As I have explained, the sinker I use is an ordinary Wet Cel or similar line. I do not at present use a sink-tip line for salmon. My sea-trout rod for sink-tip work is an 11 foot 3 inch 'Century' heavy-duty with an AFTM 6 sink-tip line. I keep by me a second reel with a fast-sinking No. 8 line, a double taper, for the special conditions I occasionally find where a very deeply presented lure is called for.

Depth of fly and all that goes into attaining it is something of a continuing preoccupation with many fly-fishers. It is possible that in thinking so much about getting down to the salmon we forget to think about why depth is necessary. In the case of the spring salmon and the autumn fish entering a cold river, it may be a question of lethargy. Cold-water fish seem unwilling to rise far to a fly. They are usually unwilling to show as they take, although a number of exceptions come immediately to mind where the water has suddenly bulged in early spring and a fish has risen to the fly (there is no other word) and taken it like a summer fish. Occasionally, visibility is an important factor. A deep, large fly is easier to see in murky water, for example. I think, also, that some salmon are stimulated by the fly as a swimming presence in the lie near them and the takes may have an element of aggression in them, especially in autumn. Having said this, I recognise that a great deal is left unexplained. Some light on the problem may come from a careful investigation of the double-reflex theory of why the salmon takes a fly at all. If the salmon takes because of a feeding reflex, and the appropriate reflex is a sea reflex in cold water and a river reflex in warmer water, we may find some kind of answer. It is true that sea feeding has some large swimming prey in it like herring, fish which will swim near the salmon at, say, four feet below the surface in the ocean. Creatures of the plankton, the crustacea, the little squid and the many other small creatures which follow the plankton and live on it are similarly subsurface food, like middle-water flies. The smaller flies fished on a floating line may represent well the river food the salmon has enjoyed as a parr – the nymphs and shrimp and hatching flies – and these are warmer-water prey, triggering off surface or near-surface rises. It is an imperfectly worked out theory but it has some explanatory power. I like it, because it explains most of the facts, which is after all what a theory is for.

Sunk line fishing for salmon is thrilling stuff. There is something delightfully tactile about it. It is a sport of tugs and pulls and unseen takes. These can be electrifying. It is also a very productive mode of fishing in spring and autumn when fish can be large, demanding and, in spring particularly, highly sought after. It is little wonder that we study to find depth in our fishing. I heartily recommend it, provided we curb our tendency to go to the extremes and sink the fly too far or persist with the sunk line too long into the warmer weather.

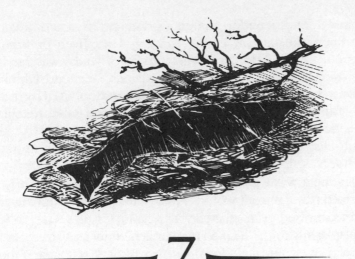

7

Signals from the Trout

I have suffered a great deal from temptation in my salmon fishing and I would like to confess that I have yielded to it many times. I refer, of course, to the temptation of trout. On a day's salmon fishing in spring you can see the first olives of the season appearing like little dark frigates on the surface of the streams and, as if waking from a kind of winter torpor, they flutter their wings and eventually fly off. Trout, also waking from a kind of winter sleep, rise to them in bursts of feeding which make the heart of any angler beat faster. There is something quite basic about this, because every salmon fisher was surely a trout fisher first and the urge to lay aside the salmon rod and flip a dry fly over the first trout of spring is sometimes overwhelming.

The temptation was strongest in my early years after salmon. I can remember fishing the Tay at Logierait just above the junction with the Tummel. The date was 29 March and we were two painfully keen young fishers given a chance day on a reasonable beat. In these early days of salmon fishing we had not much practical experience to draw on. We had read a lot,

47

looked a lot, listened to anglers talking and dreamed dreams. We knew the hearsay of the sport and we lived through a perpetual agony of longing to get into fish. That day was the first on which I ever harled – swinging a Kynoch Killer and, I think, a Toby behind the boat as we edged back and forward over the lies. Harling is, of course, the dullest form of salmon fishing ever devised and it was not strange, therefore, that we were easily distracted when trout suddenly began to rise in good numbers beside the boat.

The light was right. I could see many of the trout clearly. It seemed that the trout would hover in the water just below the surface, poised in an agitated way, waiting for flies. They would rise splashily to the flies on the surface, then, as if tired out by the activity, would sink down, or turn away, to reappear a short time later a yard or so away and rise again to the olives. This pattern of activity was fascinating. It explained, in part at least, one of the mysteries of my own early trout fishing. Trout would rise hard in a given lie and would suddenly stop, as if on whim, although flies sailed down over the lie very temptingly. This rise of Tay trout tempted me. I dived for my trout rod and set it up rapidly, only to find that the sudden and almost violent rise stopped almost as soon as I attached my leader. Typical. Why did they stop? Was it fatigue, a lasting weakness after the winter? Was there a special 'factor x' controlling them? There certainly was no shortage of flies. The Tay was covered with them.

My train of thought was suddenly interrupted. There was a distinct bump on the rod harling the Kynoch and we both pounced on it. We were into a salmon. I played the fish and it fought well, taking us well down the pool to a point where I could get ashore and finish the fight on the left bank. Trout went out of my mind as I played the fish, but I think I am right in saying that the rise started again. I was concentrating on the fish, however, and eventually led it safely over the net and grassed a fine fourteen-pound hen fish – a great prize. It had taken in the middle of a trout rise, or immediately afterwards. I have often cast my mind back to that day in spring, partly because I now believe there is a 'factor x' and that it affects salmon as well as trout. Put in another way, I now believe that conditions in spring which bring trout on to the rise also make salmon take.

On the Aboyne water of the Dee, very much more recently,

something similar happened and this early Tay incident was brought suddenly to my mind, together with all the other *Angst*-ridden times between when there had been temptation to lay aside the salmon rod and try for trout. I was on the Dee at Aboyne in early May in 1983 in what should have been the cream of weeks for floating-line fly-fishing on that marvellous river. But the spring that year was the wettest on record and instead of finding the Dee running at, say, a foot to a foot and a half on the gauge, gently maintaining its level as the snow on Cairngorm melted, I found a river running at three feet and, worse, yo-yoing daily around this high mark. It was cold, east-windy weather with blustery showers of the wettest of wet rain. Although the rules allow spinning at any height over two feet, I fly-fished – only spinning a couple of times when wind and water conditions absolutely defeated me with the fly rod. I possibly made the mistake of interpreting the Dee in flood on that occasion as more likely to produce fish to a slow-sinking line than to a floater. I had once had a memorable few days of May sport on the Birse bank opposite when the Dee suddenly rose to four and a half feet and the slow-sinking line and big flies did very well indeed. This time, however, the Dee did not respond to my deep and slow tactics, nor to the occasional sessions with floating line. I was blank from Monday to Wednesday, although the bait rods had managed four by this time.

It stopped raining on Wednesday night and on Thursday the river looked as if it might actually settle down from its 3 feet 2 inches. I also had the impression that the slight blackness in the water which the flood had brought down was lifting and the Dee was beginning to look more like its usual greenish-clear self. By lunch time I had seen fish but touched nothing on my slow-sink line. It was at lunch time that I met Sandy, the retired ghillie from the beat, a hale and hearty man in his mid-seventies, riding his new Raleigh bicycle with – wait for it – drop handlebars! It replaced his old bicycle which was described as like a field gate with wheels on it. In his youthful seventies he had bought himself a red and chrome racer with a milometer. Was there ever a better symbol of optimism and lust for life?

Sandy said, 'I don't like sunk-line fishing on the Dee. Water or no water, fish a floating line and a small fly.' Now, I am always wary of adamant advice. Sometimes ghillies advise one method because they have hardly ever fished anything else. This happens on the Tay, for instance. But Sandy's advice rang true. Also, I was rather fed up with the sunk line, seeing nothing and feeling nothing. At least the floating line would let me see some of the takes, and would give me the satisfaction of seeing the line itself fishing across the stream.

I don't know which came first that day, the feeling that all would be well or the sight of the first trout rise. The Dee is not held in high esteem as a trout water. I think this is partly justified by the adverse comparison with its neighbour the Don, which has the finest river trouting in Scotland, but I suspect that the other reason is that the Dee fishes so well for salmon with small flies that trout fishing is virtually salmon fishing and tenants pay rent for the larger fish. The feeling of well-being I felt that day was quite distinct. The river had stabilised at three feet; the water was clear; the air temperature was higher than for several days and trout began to rise well on the Bridge Pool and, as it turned out, also in great numbers on the Jetty Pool below.

I walked down from the Bridge to the Jetty, passing those lovely gravelly streams Paterson's Cast and the Stone Pool, which in lower water and in the summer give splendid fishing. I reached the Jetty, waded out a couple of steps above the top eddy and cast out my one-inch black and orange Brora Waddington on a floating line. What a splendid stream the Jetty is, rushing over gravel and forming glassy lies within the stream behind troughs and boulders on the bed. My line came round well, cutting through the rising trout as it did. The stream was faster than I would have liked ideally, but I felt strongly that, if there was a salmon in it, it would come to me. There was a sharp tug and the reel immediately spoke. A small, vigorous fish turned and shot upstream, forging through the hard water and hammering away in the stream for several minutes until it tired and came in quickly. As I played it, trout continued to rise vigorously all round the line. They seemed not to care. I was disturbing the water all right, but they did not stop rising. Extraordinary! The salmon came in and I netted it, a very fresh seven-pounder, breaking my duck for the week and reminding me that Dee fish do love a floating line.

I mentioned that the fish I had taken obligingly ran upstream, leaving the deeper lies just off the top of the jetty untroubled. There is a splendid lie there, where I had moved a salmon earlier in the week to a floating line. I swung the long line round arc by arc and was delighted by the way it was covering the lies. In conditions like this I fish off the reel, that is, keeping the rod top fairly low and keeping my fingers off the line for the main part of the fishing arc so that a salmon taking can pull as much line as he wishes in the draw. It is an excellent way to hook fish on streams. In this Jetty run, however, I had to assist the fly slightly at the end of its travel and, pinching the line lightly between my rod forefinger and thumb, I drew in a yard of slack. There was a sound like 'crump' as a salmon rose to the fly and I had a momentary vision of a good head and back. The little loop of slack snapped out and the reel immediately spoke. I raised the rod and was well into something which made the previous seven-pounder seem trivial.

It was several minutes before I saw the fish. It started by pulsing slowly in the hard water and holding well down in the deeps off the head of the jetty. Then, in a powerful run, it took masses of line and leapt. It was a superb sight, a very silvery large fish well clear of the water at the end of a long run before crashing back with a great splash into the Jetty run. I was well on to the backing by this time and my first concern was to get the fly line back on to the drum. I always feel more secure when I get a few turns of fly line back on, even if my splice has been tested, as it was that morning, and found to be perfect. The fish ran again and made another tremendous leap and then, after a deep pulling contest, leapt for the third time. All this time the trout were rising round the line. It was incredible to see the line creaming through the water, making that most exciting wild vibrating tone which you get when a heavy fish forges through a stream. But none of this disturbed the trout.

Fifteen minutes passed, then twenty, and I began to feel that hooks which had held all that pressure were probably well in and that I could lean a little on the fish and bring the fight to a conclusion. When I applied more pressure, the fish moved downstream following the outside of the Jetty stream itself, which is deep and hard into my bank. From time to time the fish stopped, faced the current and, again under rod pressure, turned and let the water take it downstream. Twice it ran out of the stream, over to the Birse side where the water is gentler, but in each case it allowed itself to be brough back. It was a tired salmon now. I got it into the big eddy below the jetty, where it toured and bored and tried twice to run out into the stream again, but I dissuaded it. Then one more wallowing tour of the eddy and I was able to slip the net under it, and the fish slid over the ring. My net is a 24-inch Gye, and of ample size for most fish, but this fish just lay there and would not bend. I did something then which I do not recommend, but it worked. I slid the net along under the fish and turned it to bag over the salmon's tail. I then netted the fish in, tail first and it bent obligingly into the net, allowing me to get my hand to the ring and haul it ashore. It was a magnificent fish, twenty-one pounds with a cluster of sea lice on its head. That salmon in those conditions is one of the best fish I have ever taken on floating line and it is some three pounds heavier than its nearest rival.

What was the meaning of the signals the trout were giving? They were saying that the whole atmosphere, the whole riverside environment was in tune. More poetically, after a week of cold easterly wind and heavy stinging rain, nature was somehow optimistic again and for an hour was reminding me what the Dee in May actually should look and feel like. Two fish in half an hour, one of which was a notable salmon, is memorable stuff. I was, as it were, looking through a window from a wet week on to the Dee in its peak form. It can give superb salmon fishing on the floating line in spring. It can also, I dare say, produce a decent trout or two in spring but I think I would be guilty of a kind of sacrilege if I were to fish for them seriously. At least that is what I feel now. But deep down I still feel, on these occasions, when trout are rising and conditions look good, a temptation hard to resist. It still happens, on the Dee, Helmsdale and Spey, but I am now very alert to the fact that rises of spring trout often signal taking times for spring salmon. I am sensitive to their messages and I am grateful for them.

Signals from the trout are environmental ones; they relate to weather, temperature, humidity and water – indeed, the whole atmosphere of the riverside. Some people have made bold attempts to describe scientifically the actual conditions affecting salmon taking times but perhaps the best discussions of the subject are in R. V. Righyni's *Salmon Taking Times* (Macdonald,

1965). The link between hatches of fly and salmon taking times is clearly made here and Righyni argues that the conditions producing a trout rise are also the conditions likely to produce salmon takes, the prime factor being availability of oxygen. Terry Thomas, in a long and interesting commentary on Righyni's case, published in the book itself, discusses the relationship between rising trout and taking salmon and, in a way which I find very close to my own ideas, looks at the whole riverside for his answers. He quotes an almost poetic dictum by the late Herbert Hatton of Hereford, a man of substantial wisdom in the taking of salmon. Hatton said that when suddenly you hear all the birds bursting into song, that is the time a fish will take. Terry Thomas has also watched trout rising in bursts and has noted that trout move at certain other times into feeding positions, sometimes fifty yards from their lies, a few minutes before a hatch of flies comes down. This he attributes to changing levels of oxygen in the river. It is not just the presence of oxygen, however; it is its availability. He calls it 'the right amount of oxygen for short periods'. Oxygen is, as I understand it, only one of the variables making conditions right for taking salmon, but it may fairly be said to be a key indicator. It is also detectable without too much technology. For me as an angler on the banks of Dee or any other water, however, taking times, signalled by the trout and by a host of other things, are marked by an indefinable sense of the moment having arrived. The signals the trout give say that everything is in tune.

8

Demythologising Mishnish

I cannot say that I grew up on the Island of Mull, but it would be true to say that, in my teens and early twenties, holidaying there and working as a student planting trees provided me with all sorts of formative experiences as an angler. Throughout this period, I was continually faced with what I rather rudely called the myth about Mishnish – that the lochs had good stocks of large trout. I had had some nice fish off their drifts, but nothing, as far as I can recall, over a pound in weight. I had another opportunity of fishing the lochs in 1982 with my good friend Ian Neale, who with his wife Jane have become incomparable fishing hosts in their fishing lodge on Mull. I had excited Ian with my talk of Mishnish when we first met, when he and Jane were thinking about settling on Mull. The tables were now turned: Ian was exciting me with his hopes for the lochs, although Mishnish had not yet produced for him one of its fabled two-pounders.

The Mishnish lochs form a small chain of waters lying almost due east and west along the road from Tobermory to Dervaig. They have always struck me as strange waters. They lie in a narrow valley in the hill above the northern end of Frisa, but they drain east through a good burn into the Tobermory river. They are three waters of different character and it does not take much imagination to see that they were separate in the not-too-distant past. A dam at the eastern end has, clearly, raised the levels of the lochs and has caused them to be linked by small reedy channels which a boat can pass through with care. The raising of the levels has also flooded what must have been marsh in the past, leaving the lowest loch a water with shallow, weedy drifts over excellent fly-bearing silt. On old Ordnance Survey maps the lochs are called Carnain an Amais (Upper Mishnish), Loch Meadhoin (Middle Mishnish) and Loch Peallach (Lower Mishnish).

These three smallish lochs run the gamut of loch types. The upper loch is distinctly Highland, with heather along its far bank and a cliffy shore on the south side. The middle loch is transitional, with shallows, and the lower loch is fertile, weedy, grassy and more like a Lowland loch than a water in the Hebrides.

We were blank for the morning, although small fish had moved to us and had either been missed or shaken off. The upper loch promised nothing. Nor did the middle loch, and it was close to one o'clock when we eased the boat through the channel into the lower loch and in calm water made our way to the eastern end – the broad, shallow, weedy end. A puff of wind rose, the forerunner of the afternoon thermal breeze. Ian tied on a size 10 Zulu on his bob. He ties them with three hackles wound round the body and produces a marvellous skidding, bobbing fly which appears to be irresistible. I had a Black Pennell on the bob, size 12. I rose a good fish and then, towards the end of the first drift, with the wind strengthening, hooked a good one, which I was witless enough to allow to weed me and break loose. Ian said something about that which I have forgotten!

The next two drifts, however, were unforgettable. The breeze seemed to alter in direction as it strengthened and we were able to drift down the southern shore of that lower loch, among columns of sweet weeds and over the excellent fly-bearing silt the loch has on its bed. Two minutes out on the drift and Ian was into a fish on his bob – a substantial fish which bent the rod hard but came to the net in time. There it was, the first really good trout I had seen taken on Mishnish. It was the sort of trout the Edwardians used to write about, but is seldom is ever met in loch fishing these days – deep, massive spots, beautifully shaped, a Mishnish two-pounder.

Was Mishnish going to show us something today? The thought had hardly formed itself when Ian's rod was in action again. The eleven-foot carbon bent alarmingly as he tried to work the fish past the mass of weeds we were in, and the pressure brought the fish up. It looked very deep, marvellously gold in colour, but shorter than the two-pounder we had in the bag. The hook held and I eventually got the net under it. It was a short, very thick and beautifully marked fish of, believe it or not, again exactly two pounds. Some average! We had to remind ourselves that we were on a ticket fishery in the Hebrides, and not a Hampshire stewpond.

I was lagging, and feeling rather cut down to size. I had not had an offer during the drift which had produced two two-pounders for Ian. I was just consoling myself for having an off day when up came a fat nose to my Pennell and there he was, boring hard, taking line and bending my rod splendidly. It was not, as it turned out, a two-pounder, but a fine fish of one pound five ounces. I had ruined the average, but I didn't feel like apologising. We landed, took some flattering pictures of Ian with his big fish, and launched the boat again. It was now mid-afternoon, and the wind was steady and quite strong. I had one eye on the time, because I was booked on the early evening ferry. Fish came well; we boated five altogether on the lower loch and not one was under a pound. At about half past four we slid back into the middle loch and gave ourselves the last two drifts of the day. The middle loch produced two close to the pound mark and gave us some splendid offers which may have been as good or better. It was going well, but I got agitated and thought I had better call it a day and catch the ferry. On the way in, cross-casting as Ian rowed, I began rising lots of trout on the upper loch, not in the same class as those of the other end but far better than we saw in the morning. I came ashore feeling that the lochs were improving all the time and might well have yielded steady sport right on until the evening brought the calms again. The seven we had weighed nine pounds exactly. It was as nice a bag as I have seen off any Scottish loch in recent years for size, shape of fish and fine markings.

I wish Mishnish were typical of West of Scotland lochs. It is not. It is neither a peaty hill loch nor a flat grassy loch, yet it has both of these elements in its make-up. It seems to me that the reason for Mishnish producing fish of this quality is the ability of the lower loch to grow snail and shrimp. The fish we took were stuffed with snail, yet had been unable to resist black bob flies worked in the wave. Looking at the setting of that lower water two things were clear. The first was the evidence of the higher level, bringing in areas of shallow but driftable water well penetrated by sunlight and full of sweet weeds. The second was the general softness of that part of the valley. I would say that the lochs had originally been formed along that high narrow valley because of glacial deposits. It was a case, in technical terminology, of interrupted drainage. These glacial deposits in the Hebrides (and also on the mainland) often bring boulder clay impregnated with shells to areas which would otherwise be peaty and acid. Lochs cut through the peat to the more alkaline clay below and we have that phenomenon – the sweet loch in what is generally a sour moor.

Mishnish is accessible, cheap and of high quality. The local club keeps it stocked and manages it well. Naturally, the water does not always do what it did for us that late June day, but on Mishnish you are always in with a chance. It is a water which, for me at least, had at last lived up to its own reputation. I headed for the ferry, delighted with the day and wondering how soon I could get back to Mull to fish the Mishnish chain again. We had demythologised Mishnish.

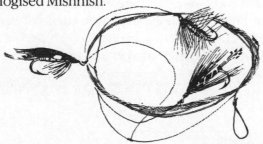

— 9 —

An Optimistic Note on Scottish Sea Trout

The first apparently fresh Scottish sea trout I heard of during the season in which this chapter was written was a three-pounder from the Helmsdale in the second week of February. The fish was examined, and although thought to be completely fresh was returned to the water during a day's salmon fishing. In the earliest weeks of the salmon season it is not uncommon to take well conditioned sea trout on the salmon fly. When trout fishing begins in mid-March, it is, again, a fairly common occurrence to hook what seem to be clean sea trout as opposed to kelts which have mended well. In fact, these very early fish are usually overwintered maiden fish on their way back down to the sea with the sea trout kelts. They are fish which, for reasons best known to themselves, have failed to mature in spawn and which return to the sea intact.

The first fresh-run sea trout may appear in March and indeed there is a Gaelic phrase describing them as the 'trout of March'. They run many of the well-known sea-trout waters of the West Highlands – the Inver, Ewe, Shiel, etc. – but are seldom caught for the very simple reason they are few in number and anglers are even fewer in number on these waters so early in the year. I have told the half-joke before that Charles McLaren, when he was a resident in Lochinver, said once that he knew of a very early April run into the Inver which numbered sixteen fish precisely. I say it was a half-joke because such a run takes place. It is a run of massive fish with their own running and spawning characteristics, which, for practical purposes, are not really anglers' fish.

Having said that, let me recall one remarkable catch some years ago taken from the peculiar little Loch Dhu on the Ailort river, which drains Loch Eilt. The keeper took three huge sea trout from this lochan on the river in very early spring. They were publicised and attracted considerable attention at the time. If my memory is correct the best fish was over fifteen pounds and two others were in the thirteen-pound class.

I have also heard it reported from Loch Maree that, when spring salmon fishing takes place in April and May, sea trout are occasionally taken on the troll and these fish are often already colouring, having been in fresh water for weeks. Again, these are large fish, part of a race of fish which is little known to anglers.

The first 'regular' sea trout show in east-coast rivers – the Spey and the Dee principally – in May. The records of the Aboyne Water of the Dee, for example, show sea trout in the bag from early May, and that is thirty miles from the sea. I usually open my sea-trout bag for the year in mid-May on that part of the Dee and often there is a big enough stock of fish there by that date to make night fishing over the tails of the pools worth while.

On Spey, sea trout are seen in April as far up as the Granton area but I have never actually been lucky enough to take one in April. By May the fish are showing in their favourite reaches as far up as Loch Insh and, by June, evening and night fishing for them is well under way. There is some indication that the runs on the Spey are coming in earlier than they did ten years ago. I would go further and say that since 1978 I have noticed a progressively earlier run, making June fishing as productive as July fishing was. There is also a very cheering sign that numbers of sea trout on the Spey (and elsewhere) are again on the increase. There have been some super Spey bags in the last couple of seasons. On one short Saturday evening in July 1982, when the light seemed very reluctant to go and I was not able to get into the pools for night fishing until 11.20 p.m., I killed eight sea trout by midnight and lost several others. It was classical night fly-fishing with a sink-tip line and two size 8 flies. What was astonishing about that magnificent burst of sport was that something happened every cast. The browns were having a go at the sea-trout fly, the rainbows (which now show up everywhere in the Nethybridge to Aviemore reaches of the Spey) were hammering away, and among them the shoals of sea trout, averaging fish of two and a half pounds, went wild over the fly.

Sea trout have shown a rising graph on several west-coast waters too, including Maree, Shiel and Loch Lomond. It seems that we are making up for some of the years of deprivation which all waters suffered in the seventies. It has been nearly a ten-year dearth, partly caused by disease. It has made many of us think carefully about the sea trout and its conservation and management. What has emerged is that sea trout, unlike salmon, are essentially local fish. Their sea feeding does not take them to the far reaches of the North Atlantic, but the selected coastal waters near the river to which they belong. Brora fish, for instance, are known to feed down the coast into the wide bay off the Fleet at The Mound. I am sure if tagging and counting operations were funded for sea trout it would emerge that every river has its own coastal feeding and, in these waters, a virtual monopoly of stock.

This means that local conditions radically affect runs into local rivers. I do not just mean that wind and weather determine sea-trout runs, I mean that any disasters, such as a big kill by estuary nets or a serious loss of stock in fresh water, will show up badly in river sport. This is a great problem, because sea trout are longer-lived than salmon. Big sea trout may be ten years old and may have recorded five spawning returns to the river. A salmon normally returns once, but it does so usually within two years of leaving fresh water as a smolt. Sea-trout smolts hang about the river estuaries, run up and down the lower reaches, show up in the sea, return within months as finnock of, say, six ounces, and as finnock may overwinter in fresh water. Think how vulnerable the sea-trout stock is as it plays and feeds and grows in the estuarial and coastal waters.

If you think of sea trout as local fish, it can radically affect how you manage them. A simple example is the protection of finnock. The small silvery finnock, which may weigh six ounces or half a pound, or if you are lucky may top three-quarters, is in fact the grilse of the sea trout. It is a fish which, within one year or less, will provide you with a mature sea trout of up to two pounds in weight. It is particularly important to protect the finnock in spring. Lots of these sprightly silver fish winter in our sea-trout rivers. They seem to arrive in any month of the year from August onwards and I am convinced that they run up during the winter closed season. Finnock which take your trout flies in March are fish which have overwintered in fresh water and are on their way down to the sea, where they will immediately begin to feed and, with luck, add anything from half a pound to a pound to their weight before returning to the river in late summer. Clearly, if we are very restrained in our finnock fishing in spring, we are likely to reap immediate sporting benefits. Unlike some longer-term conservation measures, sparing finnock in spring will bring results within the same season. I would go so far as to try, for a period of, say, five years, a complete ban on finnock fishing before mid-May.

The main sport with sea trout is, of course, divided into two broad areas – loch and river fishing. Each side of the sport has its *aficionados*. Loch fishing itself has dapping, which has all the elements of special devotion in the way its followers enjoy it, and wet-fly fishing, which is always slightly on the defensive against the more spectacular dapping, but has its many keen followers. Our ranks are marked by a special kind of neurosis, I think. Most anglers on the larger sea-trout lochs take out dapping and wet-fly tackle and worry about which to use. Dapping covers the broad drifts of Maree, Shiel, Stack and other large lochs and it has the great advantage that it shows fish to the fly, even if you miss them. Wet fly has, in my view, a far better hooking and holding record, but is significantly more hidden than dapping as a sport. You see every aerial and surface rise to

the dap, but in wet-fly fishing you might move ten fish and see none.

In river fishing, apart from lucky encounters and some spate fishing, most sea trout are taken in the dusk or the dark. What a fascinating branch of the sport this is! There is a whole science of finding and fishing sea trout at night. I am particularly interested in how sea trout move position in the pools and glides after dark. Why do they seem to prefer glides backed by trees? Why do sea trout start rising to the floating line in the evening, but then show a preference for the sink-tip, with flies only a few inches down.

It is wonderful to find sea-trout numbers in many of our waters on the increase. It is still a comparatively inexpensive form of sport, and it has great potential. It is maximally exciting and provides more action and more hair-raising thrills on light tackle than salmon fishing. We are lucky to have excellent sea-trout fishing in Scotland, and with proper local management we can make the most of this natural and sporting resource which is regenerating before our eyes.

━━◀ IO ▶━━
West Highland Sea Trout

Those who know the West Highlands in high summer and early autumn, in the peak holiday months, will know the West Highlands in one of their most public and most publicised moods. Fishing is going on everywhere. Lochs are well stocked with sea trout – unless the season has been very short of water. Rivers have sea trout and finnock in their streams and pools, grilse should be there splashing about in the rivers and salmon lochs, and you might think the menu represented Scottish game fishing at its best. It does not. The sea trout of the late summer are not a patch on those which run between the beginning of June and the middle of July. Don't get me wrong, however. High summer and autumn sea trout and occasional salmon are great fun and I travel far and often to try to get them. What I am saying is that there is a run of fish established before this which outshines those of late summer in quality and which, for me, represents the cream of the sea-trout fishing.

It is only fair to say that early sea trout do not run in very large numbers, although some years bring excellent numbers in. If you want numbers of fish, you must wait for the runs of pounders and finnock which come in during August floods. In June – if you are on the right waters in the West Highlands, say the River Ewe, or the Shiel, or on the rivers feeding any of our great north-west-facing sea-trout lochs, those short rivers draining substantial bodies of stillwater – you would see fish averaging twice the August size and individual fish of fair higher quality. In this I do not imply that quality means weight: I mean shape, condition and weight as well as sporting merit.

I used to wait until the first high tide of June before fishing seriously for sea trout in the west, and in terms of insurance this is still prudent. Fish run well before this, however, and over more than twenty years trying for these fish I have seen the runs of sea trout coming in earlier. I have also seen this magnificent run of fish seriously diminished after the disease years of the late sixties and early seventies. There are clear signs that the fish are coming back, however. Sea trout are long-lived fish, they return many times, and it may take ten years to establish again in a water system the best numbers and the right proportion of large fish to small after serious reduction of numbers. There are signs that this is in fact happening and I am optimistic about early numbers and quality again.

Early fish run the rivers of the West Highlands when the land is at its greenest and sweetest, but when the nights are at their shortest. They are almost entirely nocturnal takers, but can come occasionally and quite rewardingly during the day, especially if you get wind on the river. The exception to this is probably the sea pool or pools of a good sea-trout river where the tide and the artificial 'spate' caused by the filling of the sea pool with brackish water and the backing up of the pools immediately above this cause fish to run in and take as the pools drain out as if a spate were running off. The night fishing, however, is memorable and has something in its quality which approaches the spiritual. I have never experienced anything more serene than a soft June midnight on the Shiel with the night glowing, rather than darkening. It is not darkness, because you can see the whole glen and out to the west you can glimpse the tops of the hills of the islands. Birds sing nearly all night and

in the days before the corncrake disappeared from the West Highlands (I heard my last one in 1969) they craked all night. One, I remember, in the fields around Cliff had a throat problem. It craked (or croaked) for the first half of the call and then suddenly broke to crake octaves higher. An adolescent corncrake? Noises and scents and the sight of a whole dim landscape are the background of sea-trout fishing in June in the short West Highland nights and in this magic setting sea trout run and take the fly well.

My first Shiel sea trout was taken on such a night in the early sixties. I had been invited up to join friends who knew the river well and I was taken to see the river in daylight. The rhododendrons and azalias were in bloom beside the massive Garden Pool where the road clings to the rock as if it were cemented to the cliff face. The pool below pours in through a narrow ravine known as the Gullets and swirls round below the road to a cast called the Parapet, where, in the right conditions of water, salmon lie and can be risen to the fly by the rod perched fifteen or twenty feet above. That June the great Garden Pool was moving with sea trout. Fish showed at regular intervals all day in the deep, safe water. They were unfishable and uncatchable by day, but at night they tailed down to the narrow draw-off from the pool to Grassy Point and the stages below where the river runs sweetly over rocks, not too deep, and the trees of the gorge shade the water.

I was put on to Grassy at dusk, and was so keen to get started that I practically had to be manacled to keep me back from the water until the light drained away enough for fishing to start. I had two size 8 flies on my cast, with a Dunkeld on the dropper, and I was fishing a 9½-foot cane rod, a Sawyer Stillwater, one of the Ritz 'parabolic' rods which I was very keen on at that time. I crept round the rock on Grassy Point and cast out towards the wooden stage on the far side. The glide took the flies round splendidly and I was expecting a pull from the first moment. To make the suspense worse, every so often a fish would turn in the glide, sometimes above me, sometimes below me. The sea trout were at their favourite dusk pursuit of roving and showing. Adrenalin fizzed in my arteries. But, as if to keep me humble, it was some time before I felt anything at all. Probably I had started ten minutes too early. Then came the most delicious pull, the rod was bent into the fish and that unforgettable tight pulsing announced a fish well on. It was certainly heavier than anything I had touched in the dark before. I was used to 1½-pound fish, or with luck two-pounders, in my Ayrshire rivers. This was something completely different. The rod bucked and pulled and the reel spoke. The fish ran, leapt somewhere in the gloom and crashed about, but the hook was well in. It felt as heavy as a salmon, but far livelier, and during the fight it held on and bored harder than any salmon. From time to time it showed, shaking and splashing as I imagine one of Zane Grey's tarpons might. Then the fish quietened, began turning in circles and showed as a black line on the surface where its back came out. One of my friends netted it, a most beautiful, deep fresh sea trout of six and a quarter pounds. My first Shiel sea trout and, while not my best, one of the top ten fish I have had over the years in that lovely river.

I was very lucky to be able to get to know this river in its sea-trout-rich years in the sixties. These were astonishing seasons with heavy early fish in good numbers in June. There was a memorable atmosphere associated with the fishing. The rods settled to fishing their allocated pool or stream. I think it was the following summer that I spent one night fishing the lowest of the stages below Grassy and on the tail of the deep pool below me, the Duck Pond, my friend Oliver Williams was fishing. In these days there were no stages to help you to cover the pool tail and Oliver had carefully charted a wade out through deep mud and knee-clinging weed to reach a shingle ridge from which he could cast over some of the tail of the pool. The night was totally still. I was doing little on the stages although fish were crashing about here and there, especially on the deep, muddy holding water of the Duck Pond well over on the other side. Every so often I would hear a walloping splash, and Oliver's reel going. I think he took three, or perhaps four, in quick succession and there was not a fish under three pounds in his bag.

Even in the short nights in the West Highlands in June, there are phases of sport. These phases are very important for tactics. For example, many sea-trout evenings begin with a kind of prelude when fish will move to your flies but not take properly. Then the fish settle, often within ten minutes or so, and the dusk rise is on. The dusk and early dark merge to give you the best floating-line fishing of the night and it may be well after midnight before the next phase takes over. In the West Highlands, midnight is an early hour. Many a night will find the first dusk fishing only beginning at about half past eleven. The next phase, which is usually marked by a rather dead silence falling over the river, may not start until about half past one in the morning on these light June nights. This phase of silence is read by many anglers as the end of the night's sport and lots of fishers go home to bed then. Perhaps they are wise. After all, they might be on parade to fish for salmon the next day and all night and all day makes Jack not so much a dull boy as a totally zombie-like boy. One of my friends on the Shiel calls the state we get into when we have all-night sessions at sea trout followed by all-day sessions after salmon 'the Acharacle falling-down syndrome'. But what a way to go!

The silent phase of the night really means that you are more likely to pick up fish with a sinking line than you are with a floating line. I happened to be on the lowest casting platform on Captain's Pool on the Shiel one June night when the doldrums began. The pool was no longer crashing with sea trout, but lay black and glassy and seemingly fishless in the still of the wee sma' hours. I had my other rod set up with a sinking line, a small demon on the tail and a Dark Mackerel on the dropper. I crept on to the stage and cast the flies out on a fairly short line, letting them edge in over the weeds and into the rather muddy little basin which lies just below the stage. It was very exciting. I could see little or nothing except the inscrutable glassiness of the pool tail. Then I felt a sudden touch through my fingers on the line, immediately followed by a very strong pull, and there he was, pulling and throbbing and splashing in the dark and shattering the peace of the doldrums. I had two from that stand, one a fat four and a half pounds and one slightly smaller. Lovely fish.

I feel quite at ease in the dark when I am fishing. I feel part of the riverside and I sense nothing alien in the gloom, but some good fishers I know find the darkness isolating and threatening. It is only very rarely that you will find your hair standing on end. It happened to me on the tail of Captain's, fishing from the stage on the left bank one early July evening. It was a poor night for seat trout. I had one, not very big, and there was little activity to give me hope. The stillness of the doldrums came down over the scene like a blanket and the air felt marginally chilly. I could see the glassy glide of the tail of Captain's moving off rather mysteriously into the flats below. Suddenly the flats bulged and formed a great vee of black ripples. I thought it was a fish of monstrous proportions, a July salmon out of prehistory, with a back like a hog's. The sight terrified me for a few seconds until the intrusion resolved itself into a seal, moving up the Shiel, much to my disgust, ruining the pool for fishing and destroying the stillness of the place.

I have seen seals in many rivers and they always seem to be out of place. They shock me initially, then, as shocks often do, they release a kind of anger in me. I was fishing the top stream on beat 4 of the Lochy the autumn before writing this chapter and those who have had the pleasure of fishing that water will know that the beat ends at a rocky promontory where the river has some great hog-backed boulders in it and protruding ridges of rock while the Lochy boils in deep nasty holes below you. The cast is precarious. It is hard to get to, through trees and bushes, and it is a mountaineer's perch rather than an angler's stand when you reach it. Below you are the turbulent deeps of a great pot-hole. I would not have gone up had I not seen a fresh salmon showing there. As I fished, Spey-casting my fly as well as I could, I saw another, but, while both lies were reachable in terms of casting, neither was fishable. The intervening currents pulled the fly off course and made it hopeless. I fished down to the tail of this lie to where the water breaks over the ridge below and forms one of the headstreams of the Cat Pool. My mind was still uneasy because of the dangerous footing and the menacing pot-holes below in the rocks. As I looked, the stream parted and showed what I instantly took to be a salmon of astonishing proportions. There was, again, that moment of *frisson*, that feeling that perhaps it was Leviathan, the monster – 'Canst thou draw out Leviathan with an hook? . . . Canst thou put a hook into his nose? . . . Canst thou fill his skin with barbed irons? . . . None is so fierce that dare stir him up. . . . When he raiseth up himself, the mighty are afraid. . . . He maketh the deep to boil like a pot. . . . Upon earth there is not his like.' Some deep primitive fear was touched until the hog-back transformed itself into a seal.

Fishing has a very special intensity in it, a concentration of excitement and pleasure heightened by the anticipations and longings we have for fulfilment in it. The spectrum which produces intensity and delight at one end shades through more concentrated surges of surprise and the most adrenalin-charged side of experience into mystery and, eventually into primitive terror. In the idyllic setting of our game fishing, we seldom touch more than the curiosity, surprise and delight of it all. There lies below it all, however, a half respected world of mystery and in certain circumstances – a still dark night on the Shiel or fear of the pot-holes on the Lochy – something quite timeless in its fright, which can overtake you, the reverse of the coin of delight.

West Highland June nights also extend to lochs. While we fished the Shiel we also had occasional opportunities to fish the small loch from which the Moidart flows. It is, really, not much more than a very large pool set in a lovely glen. The sea trout of the Moidart were (and I hope still are) large. Ten-pounders were not uncommon and several in the upper teens of pounds have been taken there. One huge dead fish of nineteen pounds was once found. We used to fish that astonishing little loch in the dusk and dark. I remember starting with a nine-pounder which took my fly right at the beginning of the drift among water weeds near the outlet of the lochan. But fishing with a sinking line in the dark from a boat slowly rowed over likely water, because there is no wind there at night, was very thrilling.

I shall not forget taking a fish of about six pounds one June night and, for the first part of the fight, not seeing it at all. The sides of the glen there are steep and they blot out the sky, but looking far down the lochan, as if through a vee-sight on a huge rifle, you could see the last glow of the sunset over Kinloch-moidart. I was attached to this lively fish in the dark, not only wondering what it was, but wondering exactly where it was, when the fish ran and leapt. I saw it in sharp profile for one split second as it leapt into the vee of light between the hills. Unforgettable. I got the fish and it was everything I though it would be. It was heavy, around six pounds, deep and fresh and it had given a very good account of itself.

West Highland sea-trout nights are treasured, are longed for and, sometimes, are very rewarding. I have written elsewhere about my best Shiel bag, which came on a night which ws not doing well. It was a clear night, and the day's heat was radiating off the river and causing some steaming. I hate steaming. It is hopeless for night fishing and any quantity of it will drive me home to bed. This night the sky was hard and clear and although sea trout were there in numbers none would look at our flies under the harsh, clear sky. I was on the lower stages when, after one in the morning, a whisk of cloud came over. I was at that time fishing the long cast from the lowest stage, trying to cover the stream which flows opposite under Heathery Bank, a bluff covered with heather and backed by tall trees. I suddenly got into fish. The first was a magnificent sea trout of eight and a half pounds, which took a lot of killing and which raised my hair several times as it fought round the end of the stone pier of the stage. What a fine fish it turned out to be! I fished the water immediately after netting the big one and got another of six pounds from it. Luck was certainly changing. A virtually blank night suddenly looked like breaking records. I trotted up to Grassy Point and took a 5¼-pound sea trout on the glide. Fantastic! Down again, with the night light beginning to go and dawn starting in the north-east, and I fished Heathery Bank again and took the tiddler of the evening, or should I say morning. It weighed a pound and three quarters. There they were, four sea trout totalling well over twenty pounds. I have never had an hour to match that for quality of fish and weight. I have approached it for weight, but never for quality and never, for the sheer unexpected success of it, after a blank with sinking spirits.

West Highland sea trout are, of course, not genetically different from Spey fish, or Dee fish or any other sea trout you care to name in Scotland. They are, however, different in environment. They have the magnificence of the setting of their river or loch. They have those soft June nights, the blue remembered islands, the scents of the bog and the wispy hay and the smell of the sea. They are sentimentally different. But when they are on form, in June, they are also of a quality which makes the sport of August and September look poor by comparison.

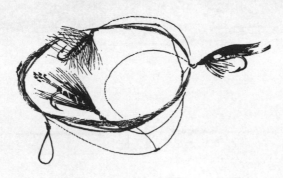

II

Sea Trout Size

Thinking about sea-trout size is not merely about specimen hunting. It is, of course, wonderful to catch individual large sea trout and I have had two or three which I remember with the greatest pleasure and which I am sure I will go on boring people about for many years to come. They are interesting in themselves, these large fish. How old are they? How many times have they run the river? What condition factor do they show? Thinking more widely on the question of sea-trout size raises different points, however. There is the question of locality – sometimes meaning not just the river or loch concerned, but the particular reach of water involved. There is the question of the type of sea-trout population in the system you are fishing, and that covers growth rates and the number of returns made by individual fish. It also covers the question of finnock – the grilse of the sea trout. I will also say something about where and how big sea trout are caught – loch or river, dapping or wet fly, day or

72

night fishing, and whether the fish are predominantly caught in one part of the year.

Let me begin with some aspects of growth rate. The rate of growth of sea trout depends mainly on the quality of the food available in the estuary. Stocks of sea trout are, to a large extent, local. Indeed, it often seems to me that this point has been ignored by some fishery managers. The salmon departs for mysterious and far-flung feeding grounds and almost as mysteriously returns to make its spawning run up the river of its birth. The sea trout, however, is hatched in the river and lives the life of a parr there, just like a salmon. It makes its downstream migration as smolt and the smolt shoals seem to dawdle for long vulnerable periods in the brackish waters of the estuary and in the sea itself just off the river. Small boys, herons, gulls and seals all must take their toll of the smolts in their vulnerable meandering in the estuary. I know a certain amount about small boys and sea-trout smolts. The smolts are silvery and six inches long, or perhaps, after a short stay in the estuary, a little heavier, and they are exciting fish for a boy to catch on fly. Locally, they are given names like yellowfins, or they may be referred to as finnock or whitling or shoal peal or one of the other local names. They are, in fact, smolts and to call them anything else tends to suggest that it is in order to kill them. It is not and any toll of smolts in the estuary is a special tragedy. The fish has managed to hatch successfully, and live for two or maybe three years in the river and reach migration size. Once the fish is in the sea, the chances of maturity and a return to the river are greatly increased. In many cases, the killing of a smolt in salt water robs the river of a twelve-ounce finnock within four months, or of a mature sea trout of anything up to three pounds one year later.

Sea-trout smolts sometimes grow at a great rate in their first year in the sea. There are cases of first-return fish to the Tweed within a year of smolt migration weighing three and a half pounds. Orkney can show similar growth rates. While most of us would be glad to see a pound or a pound and a half a year, it is marvellous to find a fast-maturing crop of fresh sea trout making more than twice this weight in one season. The factors producing large returners are environmental – that is, the quality of the estuary and coastal feeding – and genetic.

It is a kind of irony that some of the fastest-growing sea trout, like the fish of the Tweed, are very poor anglers' fish. The most remarkable cases of this, however, are to be found in the sea trout which appear in the estuaries of small fenland and East Anglian rivers. There is virtually no upstream fishing for these very large fish, yet there is an established run of them, clearly spawning successfully in some part of the river system. I have never fished for these large east-coast fish, but I have talked to some fisheries scientists about them. They seem to be coarse and perhaps even rather unattractive fish, and they seem to have little or nothing of the leaping, splashing *joie de vivre* of Scottish fish – or, should I say, of almost all Scottish fish. Scotland has its Tweed and Till fish which are not of central importance to anglers. Of course they are caught, usually in the course of fishing for autumn salmon. They are often very large – thirteen and a half pounds is the largest I have seen taken, but larger fish certainly exist. These Tweed fish have been anomalies for generations. The locals in Berwickshire call them sea dogs, perhaps as a term of disrepute. Until modern times, these large sea trout were widely known on the Tweed as 'bull trout' and were given the Linnaean Latin name *Salmo eriox*. There is, or should I say was, a very strong tradition of calling North-Sea sea trout bull trout and those returning to Northumbrian rivers, such as the Aln and Coquet, were given the name. Those of Tweed and the East Lothian Tyne were similarly named. Lamond, in his fine book *The Sea-trout: A Study in Natural History* (1916), ponders over this term 'bull trout'. He puts it in inverted commas, showing, I think, that as a biologist he was a little embarrassed by it. But he does give a clear description of what I am sure we would call a race of sea trout rather than a species.

I have not overlooked the run of heavy sea trout which occurs in our east coast rivers, a run which once again opens the 'bull trout' controversy. The Tweed netting close time, and indeed the Aln close time also, begins on September 15, and the evidence is fairly conclusive that the major part of the run of these large fish occurs after the net close season has begun, with the result that the nets take a comparatively small toll of them and their numbers tend to increase to the prejudice of more marketable fish. I cannot explain why there should be this late run of heavy

74

fish, but it seems to me that it is another pointer to the conclusion (suggested, as I have shown, by the scales) that there is a species of sea trout on the east coast that, whatever it may be classified as, is not identical with the sea trout of other waters. (p. 148)

Elsewhere in his fascinating book, Lamond makes a remarkable suggestion. He gives a great deal of space to the theories of other writers on the subject, from Walton on, and he quotes Tate Regan freely. He strongly inclines to the view that the bull trout is a race and that it is the descendant of a great prehistoric race of sea trout associated with the original North Sea river. He links the bull trout of the Tweed with the long-extinct sea trout of the Rhine. In an exciting and highly romantic paragraph he speculates that there were three prehistoric great rivers – the Irish Channel river, the English Channel river, and the North Sea river, which he also calls the ancient Rhine. Each produced its races of sea trout which displayed particular characteristics. The bull trout, so called, are the modern remnant of the great fish of the ancient Rhine. This heady and romantic notion cheers me up when I catch a Tweed sea trout. You are, I muse, my link with the beginning of the world. Thoughts like that do one a power of good on a bleak November day.

Contact with the large sea trout of Tweed is reasonably uncommon, particularly when one finds that some beats of the river are full of sea trout in autumn. I used to be in a small syndicate which fished Maxton, a beat on the Tweed near St Boswells. A small burn joins the beat from the right bank and it forms a deep bay where it joins the river inside a shingle bank. In November, there were sometimes twenty or thirty substantial sea trout lying in that small pool. I began to notice them when UDN came, and fish produced white blotches on head and back. One November day, I think it was in 1977, I looked into that pool and thought the bottom was covered with leaves. I had a *frisson* of horror when I realised that I was looking at a great collection of large sea trout, three, five and seven pounds in weight, all apparently affected by UDN. When I fished there the following week they were all gone, up the small burn I presumed. Diseased fish spawn, if they can. I hope these fish did, because, surely they were the total stock of that small water. In the years I fished Maxton, however, spring, summer and autumn, I never caught one sea trout, nor can I actually recall any ever appearing in the book.

I finished one season about that time with a 6¾-pound sea trout from Dryburgh. It was a lean, hard-bodied fish which fought strangely, twisting and threshing and leaping about. It was a poor table fish, stringy and coarse. I should perhaps dismiss this as just a poor individual fish, but I believe it is quite general for these Tweed sea trout to be like that. I did not take scales off that fish, but it could have been very old. Sea trout can live well into their teens. Charles C. McLaren, of Altnaharra, was brought up on Loch Maree and caught many remarkable sea trout there, including, in 1928, a 12½-pounder which was eighteen and a half years of age and which had spawned eleven times. He described that fish to me as a beautiful specimen and I am sure it did not let its captor down as a table fish in the way Tweed sea trout often do.

It must be clear that I have a love–hate relationship with big Tweed sea trout. I have caught a fair number of them, but never more than one or two each season. I have spent nights trying for them in what seemed to me to be ideal fly-fishing conditions, covering water known to contain sea trout, such as the Boat Pool at Bemersyde. Was there ever a better pool tail than that? The ghillie there, Eric Stevenson, the first summer he came to the beat, thought the tail of that pool looked marvellous for sea trout and after several blanks he actually got one in the dark, nine pounds in weight. He is a man with knowledge of the Coquet and its sea trout and it may be that he had some special Northumbrian luck to add to his fishing. It is significant, however, that even with individual catches of this quality few anglers persevere in night fishing for Tweed sea trout. This is partly because the run does not appear until the late autumn, except for smaller fish, and evenings are not usually right for night fly-fishing by late September. It is also because these peculiar and very large sea trout are dour in the extreme, recalcitrant, surly and frustrating. My prejudices are showing. They say the Till fish are better, but I have never crossed the border to fish for them. It is galling to think of sea trout of such weight being so poor as anglers' fish that they are virtually non-existent in the records of some beats yet are known to be in the river in considerable numbers each autumn.

─ 12 ─

Getting to Know Spey
Sea Trout

Over the past decade, the sea trout of the Spey have been
steadily establishing themselves, building up total numbers and
establishing gradations of size which indicate that the stock now
has generations of fish in it, including older fish with many
returns to the river. I must have been asleep in the sixties,
because I did not fish the Spey extensively for its sea trout,
although I fished it a great deal then for its salmon. Perhaps the
explanation is simpler than neglect. My Spey salmon fishings
were in spring – March, April and sometimes May. I did see sea
trout in April and May, but I did not fish for them at night.
Towards the end of the sixties, however, and through the
decade which followed, I was invited to fish one of the higher
beats of the Spey, above Nethy Bridge, sixty miles from the sea,

and, much to my surprise and delight, I found it to hold excellent sea trout. I still marvel at this. Spey sea trout seem to forge all this distance up to the higher reaches of the Spey from the very early summer on, and from the reports I have been getting it even appears that the bulk of the fish taken in the river are from Grantown and above. I make one exception to this. The Avon (A'an) has a fine run of sea trout and it provides some wonderful sport in summer. The Feshie also runs good sea trout. It may well be that these two tributaries carry the bulk of the stock of sea trout for the middle and upper river. Again, a possible explanation why some well-known beats in the middle and lower river do not show big returns of sea trout might simply be that, as salmon beats of note, the rods do not fish their sea trout by night. The sea trout of the upper-middle Spey certainly go as far as Loch Insh, but not in great numbers. Members of the Grantown-on-Spey angling club do very well with the fish in June and July and after this date, while fresh fish do arrive regularly, it is largely a coloured stock of sea trout we are covering. The best fishing is between the middle of June and the middle of July, however, and undoubtedly the best way to take the fish is by fly fished in the dusk and dark. But, before actually deploying the techniques which do well on any beat, it is vital to sort out where the shoals of sea trout lie in your beat and how they behave during the hours of dusk and dark when fishing is best. On a beat I know well there is a large corner pool, deep and slow with a great reedy backwater on the left side where the pool loses pace before turning slowly round and gliding faster and faster over its sandy tail. There is a good stock of sea trout nearly always showing in the deepest eddy on the unreachable far bank. As dusk falls the fish first move up into the stream which feeds the pool. It is not a fast stream. Typical of this section of the Spey, the whole river seems to glide down into the pool below over shingle and silt. The sea trout like the extreme left bank of the pool and it is a deep, dark wade at night to get on to the middle ridge of the river and fish this place. Later in the evening, fish can also be taken on the sandy tail of the pool a hundred yards downstream and round the corner at right angles. Again it is a longish wade and each season you do not quite know what to expect. The sand becomes sculpted in a different way after each winter when the floods scour the pool out. I like this tail in the pitch dark for two reasons. First, the fish seem to tail back into it rather later than you would expect on a smaller pool; and, second, the deep, dark wade at the head of the pool is troublesome in the deepest darkness, especially if fish have to be taken ashore.

The key to knowing a sea-trout beat is partly finding where the stock rests during the day. Sea trout like a deep hole and some of the places on the slow-running upper-middle Spey which I fish are deep enough to drown a double-decker bus. In this sea trout are quite unlike salmon, which, on the whole, prefer shallower water to lie in, day or night. Sea trout are always worried creatures, it seems to me. They are agitated and fast and twitchy and insecure. I looked over the bridge at Boat of Garten in July 1983. The water was clear and the light was with me. As I peered down, I was conscious of pairs of sea trout, or little groups of fish speeding around the pool, very unsettled and acting as though they had been grossly disturbed. In fact it was a Sunday and nobody was fishing. Also, that pool has reaches where no angler could wade. Other holding pools in the area are alive with leaping and showing fish during the day. They splosh, they leap straight and high, they cart-wheel and they lunge. They are doing this in deep, secure water, for example in deep eddies in sandy holes where no angler would be able to fish properly, or would bother to. Yet the sea trout flash and leap there all day. But when the evening change comes, and the light begins to go, and that gentle dampness comes into the air as dusk approaches, the splashing in the deep holding lies stops, or at least becomes significantly less. That is the time the sea trout take first of all to the headstreams and afterwards to the pool tails. They still tour around the pool, but they lie longer and steadier in the streams the more the light fades. They are wary of the thin tails of the holding pools until the light really goes, but then, in the quietest mood they have in twenty-four hours, they lie in cool, gliding water and will take your flies.

Getting to know any river is essentially getting to know where the fish lie by day and how they populate the fishable water at dusk. I write in the following chapter about the touring and roving which sea trout show in the dark. This is a highly important aspect of the fish. It is not enough to know the routes the fish take. It is essential to know where the hovering points on these routes are and where the fish may be tempted. There is something akin to running salmon in this. You know where salmon run on many pools, yet it is only when the fish stop, even for a short breather, that they will take your fly. Sea trout on the move are not takers. As darkness falls the fish change their routes and begin to stop a little, then hover more and more. I have often been fascinated by the stability of the sea trout in the light of dawn. At that time the pools are absolutely quiet, yet a careful fly over the tails of pools can be outstandingly effective. I have been blank on the Spey all through a summer night and have persevered to take four fish from a still tail glide at half past three in the morning.

Some characteristics of sea trout are common to almost all the waters I have fished. They love hovering under bankside trees. I often wade well out into a pool tail to be able to get my flies to pull off the very edge of the glide under trees. I dare say it is darker there and it may be that the covering makes the fish feel more secure. They also love hovering beside reeds. Again I can think of a couple of places where the deepish water runs quietly round a bend beside a reed bed. In one place, the only way to get at the fish is to use a boat and anchor it, then cast a longish line right into the reeds and pull the flies off. What takes you get there! It can be quite marvellous sport. You would think that fishing from a single point like that, either by wading or by anchoring the boat, would allow you to take only one or two fish, and that the others would be disturbed. Sea trout are a little like rainbows in the way they move through the pool, however. They come to you. The secret is to know that the fish not only move past that point, but hover there.

There is no substitute for close observation of a beat on which you are to wade and fish in the dark. On one of the most successful reaches of the Spey, where the beat has a fine holding pool at the top and a deep holding bend in the middle, it is curious to find that sea trout hardly ever show and are very seldom taken in the pools or streams below the holding lies. These lower pools may look good, but it appears that the sea trout are very much shoal fish and have the fishy equivalent of the herd instinct. The presence of good pools is not enough. There must be a shoaling place. Once a shoal has started, others join. Thus a beat may have a couple of big holding lies and blank pools nearby which are hardly worth wetting a fly in. Spending an hour or two in daylight to locate the shoals is essential. The next stage is predicting where the early evening sport will be and which pool tail the fish will slide back into as darkness deepens.

There is a fine pool on one of the beats I fish which has an island at its tail. It is a hard wade to get to it, but I know the way now. Once on the tip of the island, you can wade straight up into the pool above, on a safe sandy bed. From this point you can turn and fish gently down the left or the right draw-off, because the island blesses us with two tails. I have said that the bed is sand. This means that from one season to the next you do not really know which side will be the best. I discovered one season recently that my favourite glide on the left bankside no longer seemed to have a fish in it, while the right glide-out had deepened and was by far the better place. Another season will restore the left glide-out and may silt up the other tail. That pool has a fine steady headstream and years ago I could always get a sea trout there at dusk and, on occasion, in the dark. For some reason, although the fish show well in the glide, I have not had a sea trout there for years.

Equally interesting are the pot and glide above this, where a burn comes in on the right bank. Sea trout and some grilse have always shown there and I have spent, in past years, many an hour trying for them but without much success. I think I got one once. Two seasons before writing this chapter I saw fish moving in the lie off the burn mouth and I trotted up and at dusk cast a short line out over it. I had three fish, one after the other. The following season I could not get any off that lie, but, using the boat to place me upstream of the burn, fishing a glide easily covered from the bank but always unproductive from that standpoint, I killed half a dozen one night.

From what I have said already it must be clear that, even on a beat I know well and have taken a considerable weight of sea trout off, there are annual variations which take me by surprise. I don't know how to advise you about this, except to say that there is no substitute for curiosity and experiment. Watch for fish showing in unusual places and try to predict where they will settle and glide about in the evening. Be ready for the anomalies. It may be that one bank is too close to the path of the sea trout and only wading in from the other will get them. Sea trout like a long line and like to have their privacy. They are not often caught when the rod is right on top of them. They don't mind wading, or at least, they don't mind an angler wading in and settling. Yet, even after the commotion of playing a fish and netting it, and going ashore with it, I have had sea trout within a few subsequent casts. This must be because the fish move quickly into glides after disturbance and have no knowledge of the fight that has just ended.

Getting to know the Spey, or specific parts of it, is slow work, but without it your bags will be of chance fish only. On the Spey I regard four fish in the evening as a good bag, and twice this number is a bumper bag. There are nights when you can do better, but they are not common. Remember, you will rise and miss sea trout, inevitably. A night of eight may mean encounters with at least a dozen fish. It is a very brisk piece of sport. When fresh sea trout arrive, if you are there on the right night, you might well take twenty. If you do find that you are there on a big night, my advice to you would be not to move much. You may feel that you want to give the tail a rest. A short trip to the headstream or to the glide coming down into it from the pool above is worth while. But do not fish all the pools down, as you might do for salmon. Concentrate on the taking places and stay put, or, to be Irish, as put as you can. When fish have been really on, I have on occasion invited someone to come and stand beside me and fish the same water. It works well and it is an ideal thing to do for a young angler. More can be learned by being there and getting direct advice than by any amount of talk before or after the night. Just make sure, however, that your companion can handle his rod well in the dark. Some people just can't do it and are menaces to themselves and to all and sundry. If you can't handle tackle in the dark you should keep off sea-trout fishing. For instance, you should be able to hear if the cast is clear of tangles as you cast it. You should be able to change casts rapidly in the dark. I put the old ones inside my cap and roll the new one off a card. Nevertheless, I carry two rods ready set up – one with my floater on it and one with my slow sinker or my sink-tip on. If my floater gets messed up I can either change the cast or take up the other rod. What you do not want to do is to take out your hand lamp and sort out a major tangle. The less artificial light you have on the water the better. I like netting fish by what light there is in the sky and I never wade with the help of a torch. It is useless anyway. Sea-trout nights on the Spey, while not as light as those in the Hebrides, are by no means totally dark. Let your own night vision adapt itself to the night and you will see rises and movements and takes and rod-top angles and all that is necessary for good fishing. You will also see the fish well enough to make a decent job of the netting. Getting to know yourself in the dark is vital to the whole sport.

13

Night Sea Trout: A Revised Manifesto

Nearly twenty years ago, in the sea-trout-rich sixties, I wrote a series of articles about my approach to sea trout at night and I condensed this into a chapter in a book I wrote in 1969, *A Gamefisher's Year*. I called the chapter 'A Sea Trout Manifesto'. A great deal can happen in twenty years and, re-reading my thoughts of the sixties in the middle of the eighties, I think that the time has come to try again to set down how I think myself into my sea-trout fishing. I have had some marvellous times in recent years night fishing for sea trout, fishing different waters from those I had access to in the sixties. Clearly much of what I said in the first manifesto still stands; indeed, I would be disturbed to find that any of the core ideas had altered radically. Many of the details have changed, however, and much of my fishing has benefited from spending an unreasonable number of nights on the river instead of in bed, like normal folk. One thing remains unchanged in me, however: I am still absolutely fascinated by sea trout in the dark and would go almost anywhere to fish fly after sunset for these most remarkable sporting fish.

Sound advice to any dusk and dark sea-trout fisher is not to approach the pools and gentle glides too early. Generally speaking, you should not go on to the pool tails until the light has slipped away to such an extent that you have to hold a fly up in silhouette to attach it to your cast. In June, in the West Highlands, this might not be until 11.30 p.m. In July you might be able to fish by 10.30 p.m. and in August correspondingly earlier. It is not the time on your watch which will determine the start; it will be the kind of light the particular evening brings you. The late Moray McLaren had a picturesque way of putting it. In a passage in a book we wrote together, *The Fishing Waters of Scotland*, he wrote:

> Up till well after eleven thirty at night (GMT) the colours by the loch-side held strongly and, indeed, seemed to grow brighter. Then the evening rise fell off and with its departure the colours on the land lost their strength. The grass grew grey, the purple of the uplands took on a slightly different grey and even the bright yellow blooms gave up the struggle to display themselves; the few red flowers just drained away their blood. It was a monochrome landscape.

I believe in starting my sea-trout fishing in this monochrome landscape and, as the blacks deepen and the greys become more dense, my confidence grows.

Anglers, like me, who have spent nights fishing in monochrome will know what all this means. The glides have a black and silvery look and sea-trout moves can often be seen on this surface as silver lines spreading on the surface. When the night brings darkness proper to the river the glides turn grey, a slate-like colour, giving them the appearance of a density far heavier than that of water.

A sea-trout evening need not necessarily wait until the darkness finally descends if you have streamy water to fish. Many a sea-trout evening starts with a fish or two taken on a trout cast fished down the broken streams. Sea trout in the earlier evening can sometimes be taken in the fastest glides. I started one evening in 1983 on a very fast rush at the head of the Red Brae Pool on the Aboyne water of the Dee – a pool so fast that it can only really be fished when the Dee is bare-bones low. That glide was so fast that it was difficult to stand in the foot or so of water it carried in a rush to the stream below. I cast my fly in, really to wet it and get some line out so that I could cover the decent lies on the far side, where boulders gave the fish some shelter. A sea trout seized the fly as soon as it hit the glide and I was taken a little off balance. I did manage to raise my rod and I did manage to keep in contact with the fish, despite several very high leaps in the fast water, making the reel sing. I got the fish ashore, a nice two-pounder. As the light weakens, and long before the main pools and glides are ready for fishing, sea trout can give good sport in the rushes and streams.

It is extremely satisfying to start the evening with a fish before the light has gone. If you fish a two-fly cast at that time of evening, and if you go a pound or two heavier than the trout cast I recommended above, you might well pick up a grilse or salmon. I usually put something like a one-inch Stoat's Tail tube on the tail, or a similar summer double, and this not only takes sea trout in the faster water, but takes many a salmon too. The Dee and the Spey are both splendid waters for suddenly surprising you with an evening grilse before you start the main sport of the night – sea trout.

Beware, however, of producing tension between your wish for a salmon and your main purpose – to take a sea trout. A different frame of mind is involved for each fish. The salmon calls for you to hold your flies over lies, to make the fly dwell, as it were, where the salmon are. Sea-trout fishing is much more a sport in which the fly is moved and the sea trout is far more likely to chase and take than the salmon. Equally, try not to let the odd chance of a grilse or salmon dictate heavier tackle than is necessary for sea trout. I always feel I have robbed myself of sport when I fish salmon tackle in the evening and find myself playing a sea trout on a rod which does not show the fish to its best advantage. You can always, or nearly always, make a decent job of a salmon on a good ten-foot single-handed carbon rod, and feel good about it, but you cannot make a two-pound sea trout perform well on a twelve-foot double-handed rod. Salmon are located fish, in known lies, but in the dusk and dark sea trout are much more opportunistic fish, likely to be picked up in odd places in a stream or glide as they rove.

The second part of the evening, therefore, starts when the

light dictates that you can try the tails of the pools. On most evenings, this corresponds with that period of gentle stillness which marks the coming of dusk. The humidity increases and the wind drops. After darkness falls, you might well find a small night wind rising, but there are few evenings when the wind does not ease off and calm down, as the light goes. Wind and light are often in sympathy. This is, in the main sea-trout months of June, July and August, floating-line time. Sea trout show in the dusk rise and they are best taken on a floating line. It is delightful sport. You see fish moving in the tails and in the glides. Sometimes it is the swirling turn you see, or the veeing of fish roving, or, best of all, the rising of a fish which has decided to hover for a short time in the tail glide or in the gentle carry of water which you get under the trees on the opposite bank.

The third phase of the night sport comes when darkness has really settled in and it may appear that the night rise has ended. Fish do not show as they rove; fewer fish rise, or none; you get fewer touches, or none at all. This is the part of the night I like to call the doldrums. The Scots word for this part of the night is the 'huwdumdeid' – the quiet, deep darkness which folds you in like a cloak. During this phase of the night, I sink my flies, either by using a sink-tip or a slow-sinking line. It is fascinating sport. You do not see the takes, but, as your flies come slowly round in the deep darkness, there is a telegraphic pull, or a pluck, or, strangely enough, a lightness which comes into the rod hand, probably caused by a following take.

A fourth phase of the night is undoubtedly the dawn. It reverses the trends. The monochrome period comes slowly out of the gloom, the birds sing, then the first colours show dimly. It is interesting, however, to see that in the stillness of dawn sea trout are usually firmly established in the tails and glides but do not seem to rove much. They are located, as it were, and not restless. I have often found the sink tip working well through the dawn and into near-daylight, before the sea trout leave the lies and go back as the light arrives to the safety of the pools.

The last phase of all is, predictably, the rough water and the broken headstreams, and, like the evening, you are in with a chance of a salmon again.

One of the things I have become very interested in recently, which hadn't occurred to me in the sixties, is that there is a pattern to how sea trout move in the pools at night, and understanding this can give us the key to successful fishing for them. Sea trout are restless creatures by day. They splash and lunge and show in the safe lies and the deep holding reaches of the pools. They may show incessantly in deep unfishable eddies. I know one on the upper-middle Spey near Aviemore where acrobatic and spectacular boils and lunges seem to go on all day. They stop as the evening brings the dusk, for the very good reason that the fish are at that time leaving their safe pots and first nosing up through the headstreams, then peopling the tails and the long glides.

In the dusk and dark I like to think of two types of movement. The first is roving, which is the name I give to the fish urgently and slightly nervously touring the pools, often right down into the gentle pool tails, showing or bulging, or, in shallow water, veeing the surface. Fish have roving routes and if these can be worked out you can intercept the sea trout at the right places on the routes. The first roving as the dusk comes is often fast and very unsettled. I have often watched excitedly on Highland pools as the sea trout speed into the pool tails, turn, and dart about, as if chasing something. They are not in fact in pursuit of anything. They are just unsettled and are nervous of the shallows. In a short time, the unsettled arrowing of the tails will stop and the fish will hover at certain spots in the tail, first for short times, then for longer periods. When they move again they seem to run up the roving route and, at certain points on it, hover again for fairly short periods. As the night darkens, the hovering extends and when the night settles in sea trout will take up lies in the tails and in the roving routes which they may well hold until the dawn comes.

I cannot really give you a rule of thumb for finding the critical hovering points, apart from the obvious turning points in the run-off of the tails themselves. Take the ten yards or so of water above the draw-off of the pool as likely territory and fish carefully. Keep back off it if you can. If you have to wade to fish it, wade early and stand still. Move, as the ghillie said, 'as if you were growing'. There is nothing quite so unproductive as wading in and wading out and splashing, sending off warning waves and all the negative things which characterise inexperienced wading. If I can, I fish from the bank. Where I have to wade, and I have to do it a lot, I plan my wading routes in daylight and, once into the glide, I stay in for as long as I can, unless there is clear evidence that I have read the water wrongly. Sea trout are a little like rainbows. If you stand still in a likely spot, roving and hovering fish will bring the sport to you.

I said I could not give rules of thumb for many of the hovering spots for sea trout at night. But I can describe one or two that I have taken scores of fish from and they may give you a clue on how to read your own water. On the Spey I am sometimes given the chance to fish a beat with good sea trout. On one large pool the tail is divided by a well consolidated island. The island has been there for as long as there have been maps of the river, but the spit of sand and shingle which runs up into the deep pool above the island changes regularly. Sometimes it will spread to the left bank and make the left half of the split tail too shallow for good fishing; sometimes it will be gouged out on the other side to form a deep channel. The whole of the sandy glide on each side works well in most years, but it is essential each season to check on what the spring floods have done to the bed. On the left bank opposite the tip of the island is a piece of the bank under scrub trees where cattle have formed a muddy drinking place. I have often found that to be the best hovering point on the whole tail. Simply, the cattle have formed a little bay and its headland has caused the stream to dig out a small hollow. Sea trout lie there and it can be deadly. I know another on the same beat where a long wade takes you to a reach in which a dead tree lies. Fish rove up to this point and wait there, but they go further and I have sometimes found them in good numbers just above the dead tree in the gentle apron formed there beside the headstream. Note that this is a hovering point well away from the pool tail. Indeed, the pool itself is huge and turns a right-angled bend there. Fish seem to rove the whole length of the pool, but they are seldom caught except at the extreme tail or in the hovering lies around the dead-tree reach.

Roving routes and hovering points are special, local information and you may well find that you have to take the time to work them out for yourself. One tip: do not assume that showing points are hovering places. I would far rather fish a couple of yards above a showing place, or a couple of yards below. A showing fish is often in the process of moving, and I suspect that these fish, if they take at all, do so with a pluck or a pull which often comes to nothing. The hovering fish make sure of the fly.

These two points – identifying phases of the evening sport and studying roving and hovering – are essential parts of a productive philosophy of sea trout. It is uncanny how quickly you develop a 'nose' for spots. I love glides under trees on the far bank. On the middle island stream on the Irvine House water of the Border Esk it is a fairly long cast over to the bushes on the island, but there, in tne gentle water almost under the branches of the scrub trees, are several first-class hovering places. I far prefer those to the lies in the tail of that stream. Everywhere I see a similar pool, that one comes back to me as a pattern and, largely, it works. I know a Spey pool where trees were cut down and the sea-trout fishing at that point went off badly. Sea trout love trees by the water and they hover well beside them. My sea-trout fishing, as far as locating fish goes, has become one of superimposing images of well-known pools on new ones. I slide a known pool on to the new one, like a wet transfer. Very few pools fail to respond.

Choosing the Right Fly

Sea trout in the dusk and dark like a good mouthful. It is perfectly true that sea trout will take trout flies in daylight and, if you fish these smaller flies, say size 12, into the dark, you will still catch a certain number of fish. There can be little doubt, however, that sea trout like a fly with size and bulk in its dressing. In recent years, I have narrowed the choice down to a few highly successful shapes and patterns of fly.

The basis of a good night sea-trout fly is the hackles. I am not absolutely sure whether hackles on the fly are favoured because they are better seen by the fish in the dim light or whether they produce a better 'blip' in the water in the dark, rather as certain materials like foil can produce a radar image disproportionately larger than the bulk of the object. I incline to believe that it is detectability, rather than visibility, which characterises a successful fly.

Let me list three patterns which have caught many sea trout

for me. The first two listed, the Black Pennell and the Soldier Palmer, have as many hackles tied in palmer-style as can reasonably be tied in. Hebridean Pennells and their bulky relative the Black Zulu are often dressed with three or four hackles in their bodies. They are dressed mainly for fishing sea-trout lochs by day, but also very useful night flies. These large flies are outstandingly successful in Highland and Hebridean fishing. At the extreme, think of each pattern tied for dapping. I was sitting in a boat on a Hebridean loch early this summer trying for the first sea trout. The dapping fly used, tied on a tube, carried eleven large hackles. It was enormous – a sweep's brush of a fly. Yet it is to just such bulky patterns that sea trout come by choice. These very bulky patterns are not what I would choose for river night fishing on, say, the Spey or Dee or Shiel. I like my night flies to have presence and movement and bulk is not a prime demand.

I shall not give the dressing of the Black Pennell and the Soldier Palmer, since these flies appear in most fly-dressing guides. I will, however, describe and give the dressing of my favourite night fly for sea trout which is not generally known and, as far as I know, is tied only by Dickson's of Edinburgh. It is the Dark Mackerel, invented by David Leslie of Dickson's, first as a trout fly, but – perhaps because I found it brilliant as a sea-trout fly and have written about it for about twenty years – now much-used as a sea-trout fly. It is dressed with a claret lurex metal body with a claret hackle wound down the body in palmer style. The wing is dark mallard. And there it is, a simple straightforward fly looking like a relative of the Mallard and Claret. It has presence if not bulk; it has glint, if not glitter; it has sobriety of hue. Best of all, this fly has my confidence. This means that I expose it nearly all the time to sea trout and, as a result, find that its success is reinforced – the usual spiral of confidence. If you were to limit me in salmon fishing to a Stoat's Tail and in sea-trout fishing to a Dark Mackerel I would chuckle. It would not be a limitation at all. It would be a release from anxiety about pattern choice – a freedom from *Angst*.

What I would like to advocate, however, is that the sea-trout flies one fishes ought to be tied in different styles. For example the straightforward size 8 single fly is fine, although I have always found it best tied on an outpoint hook. The best used to be Dickson's (and Martin's) outpoint singles, made originally, I think, by Sealey. These disappeared from the market some years ago and, although I had bought as many dozens as I could find, the time came in the seventies when they ran out. Fortunately Partridges came to the rescue and produce splendid outpoint singles and trebles. I have used little else since the rediscovery.

I have tried Dark Mackerels in size 8 and size 6 singles and the smaller size works best. I have had them tied up in doubles and I am not wholly convinced that they do any better than singles, although for day-time salmon fishing with a single fly the low-water double is a great fly. I occasionally fish a double on the dropper at night, but it can be a distressing fly for snagging the net, itself, the angler and any other thing around. It does take fish, however.

As an aside on this problem of fishing two flies in the dark (which I do all the time) and facing the hazards of snagging, during a highly successful late-June evening for sea trout on Spey, with seven fish already in the bag, – I saw a splendid fish splashing at a hovering place well known to me. I covered the fish and thought there was a move, but felt nothing. I rested the lie for a few minutes, by trying a lie two yards further up; then, lengthening line again, I covered the place where the big fellow had shown. There was a massive pull and I was into him. He shook the cast like a worrying dog and ran hard up and down the reach. I was wading well out on a sand spit above the tail glide and, as is my practice there, I let the fish use all the water round me in the fight, keeping an eye on my rod top to see in which direction the fish was heading. This fish came in after a while, and circled me tiredly. I unhitched my net and reached out to get it into the water ready for drawing the fish over it. I felt the gentlest of touches and knew at once that I had miscalculated in the dark and had snagged the double Dark Mackerel in the meshes of the net. The fish felt it too, and made a weak sweep round me. I was forced to turn and follow it with the net snagged in as part of the fight. Ghastly! But the fish was really beaten. I walked it gently in front of me into the shallower water. Switched on my lamp – something I rarely do in netting – and saw the great form of the sea trout lying exhausted on the golden sand of the river bed. Taking a deep breath, I released rod pressure and folded the net round the sea trout and got him ashore. I was very, very lucky. It was the best fish of the night, four and a half pounds. Doubles on droppers – indeed droppers themselves, although they take many fish – are not without their hazards in the dark.

On the tail I prefer the Dark Mackerel dressed as a Waddington. The body is about an inch long and is armed with a tiny outpoint treble, size 14, which I allow to dangle without a stiffener. This design of the Dark Mackerel provides nice trailing strands of mallard and, although it is not a bulky dressing, it as hackles wound down the shank and it has excellent presence.

This particular dressing has a great advantage: it holds the fly gently down under the surface. I have never really taken to the surface lures Hugh Falkus has had such success with. Perhaps there is still time for me to be converted. What I have found with the sea trout I meet on the Dee, Spey and other waters is that the fish show fear of the surface on still summer evenings and many fish take the Waddington-style Mackerel when it is just under the surface with no visible surface rise. How well these little trebles hook fish! They also hook the net well, of course, and netting a fish on the dropper in the dark almost always means that the tail fly snags the meshes of the net, which can be infuriating. I have on several occasions cut off the snagged fly, replaced it with a new one on the point of the cast and later, next morning for instance, have unsnagged the offending treble.

Depth of Presentation of Fly

I have already mentioned that I like fishing floating line in the first part of the evening, but my preference is for a fly slightly under the surface of the water, rather than right on top. There are occasions, for example on the Border Esk, when skittering a dropper works well, but I have perhaps lost the art of this in recent years, because I tend to get offers and fail to hook them. The fly two or three inches down, but fished with a fully floating line, makes a clean job of hooking and holding fish. On the June night I have mentioned, I took eight fish, lost two and pulled two others. In summer sea-trout fishing, that is a high proportion of fish touched and eventually netted. I believe this is the result of fishing, as it were, the *undersurface* of the glide rather than the surface we see from above.

Sunk flies account for excellent sea trout when the fish go off surface or semi-surface presentation. On some waters, principally the gentler waters one finds on dams, on slow Highland rivers in their moorland stretches, and even on lochs at night, sunk flies are the only method which will bring fish to the net. How deep should they be fished? I have experimented with flies immobile on the bed or nearly so and have caught fish, including some very large sea trout up to ten pounds. On reflection, I do not think this really is legering a sea-trout fly, as I described it in the sixties and seventies. The sea trout is a rover. As he moves he disturbs the water and raises flies from the bed or from the lower reaches of the glide. I think moving sea trout make the flies swim and they or their followers take them as they move. I cannot conceive, now, of sea trout picking flies up off the bed, in the way reservoir anglers in England describe rainbows picking up lures which are left lying on the bottom.

The halfway house – the sink-tip line – can be excellent for sea trout both in the evening and in the deep-line phase of the night. I prefer it to the sinking line, although the slow-sinking lines which settle into the water rather than sink through it are close rivals and attract me very much. I was delighted to see such lines appearing again on the market recently. These lines, my older friends remind me, replicate silk in their sinking characteristics. History repeats itself.

A manifesto leaves a lot unsaid. It is supposed to be a statement of principles and intentions. I have bent the idea a little to make it embrace beliefs, and practical approaches to sea-trout fishing. With a wild, rather mysterious living fish like the sea trout – a migratory fish of two environments – beliefs can be demolished easily. Length of stay in fresh water alters their character; residence in one pool produces educated fish. But the core of my manifesto is what has actually worked for many years on a variety of Scottish waters. It is intended to provide a statement of a solid nature, while never advocating either that these are the only successful ways of catching sea trout or that a further decade might not add dimensions to our understanding of the fish and of the ways of angling for it successfully.

14

Salmon in the Dark

I do not specifically fish for salmon in the dark. In the dusk, yes, but not seriously after the night finally comes. On the Dee, for instance, in mid-May and early June when it is bright overhead, your best chance of a fish might be in the gloaming as the light drains away. On late Dee evenings, I consciously tackle up for the chance of a dusk salmon when I make up my sea-trout cast. This usually means, in Dee terms, tying on something like a one-inch Stoat's Tail tube fly on the tail of a two-fly cast. The dropper above it might be a size 8 or a size 10 Black Pennell, Dark Mackerel or Soldier Palmer. Sea trout often take the dropper, but occasionally a salmon takes the tail fly. How occasionally? I expect a couple of salmon per season on my sea-trout flies. The Aboyne water on the Dee, which I have a regular beat on, shows perhaps a dozen fish taken each summer after 11 p.m. While many Scottish nights fall into what the Scandinavians call 'white nights' – that is nights when the light

never really drains away and dusk seems to merge with dawn – it is still not unusual to take a salmon in complete darkness.

Being split between salmon and sea trout can be a source of tension and inefficiency in dusk and dark fishing. Indeed, sometimes salmon which take the fly in the dark can be a nuisance, as happened to me on the Dee at Birse on a June night in 1982. Birse has, down near its lower march, a pool called McKidd's. It is named after the memorable character Willie McKidd who was head ghillie on Birse for many years and who ruled the roost in a way which left no one uncertain of his wishes. He had a touch of Falstaff about him – not a little of the gentle rogue mixed with a special kind of authority. McKidd had discovered his pool after a flood had gouged out a deep lie in a stream behind the large island formed at the bottom of the Birse water. To get to the island you have to wade fifty yards or so through the bottom of the Island Stream, quite a fast piece of water if the Dee has anything at all on the gauge above summer level. At a foot it is still possible, but certainly not advised above that, not only because of the wading, but because the pool itself fishes best when the rest of the river is down to its bare bones. Once you reach the tip of the island, a large well-treed piece of land, you find McKidd's Pool at the head of the right-hand channel – a fast, deep run which has scoured out a fine pot below a tree stump. The stream runs fast into the island bank right at your feet and is shallow under the trees on the main bank opposite. It is marvellous low-water salmon fishing. On the night I am describing the Dee was a trifle too high, but the pool was full of sea trout.

I waited for the light to dim. Several salmon showed in the stream, but under the trees and down near the tail several sea trout showed with that characteristic plop the fish make. I was raring to get my fly over them. I thought the stream was strong enough to demand a cast anchor – a slightly heavier fly on the tail to prevent skating. I often use an unweighted tube on glides on the Dee but in this weight of stream a Parker tube or any similar fly tied on a polythene body would have been washed away, so I tied on a size 6 Sweep single and above it, on eight-pound nylon, I mounted a size 8 Soldier Palmer.

Sport began at once. I had a pluck, then a solid take in the stream, and I netted a sea trout of two pounds. I was in again and got into a second sea trout which shook out the hooks after a good fight which bent my eleven-foot carbon rod well. My sea-trout blood was up. The night was terrific and even if the water was slightly too fast I was managing to get into fish. At that point I had a solid pull and, wondering at first if it was a sea trout of some size, I waited for the first run and leap. I got it but there was no doubt in my mind then that I was into a salmon around the twelve-pound mark.

It was hard to objectify my feelings. It had been a hard spring and I was very short of fish. It had also been a hard week, and I had not grassed a fish. But the negative side was that this pool was full of sea trout. The one on the bank was the first good fish of the season and I knew that there was a chance that the pool would fish well into the night. I could only hope that the salmon would fight hard in the stream and kill itself quickly so that I could get back to sea-trout fishing. Well, it did fight well. It ran hard and it showed several times and, really, gave me good sport. After ten minutes I felt I was getting the upper hand, but the fight dragged on for another ten, with the fish alternately showing signs of being tired and finding amazing reserves of new energy.

I was, as I explained earlier, on a steep island bank with a fast, deep, unwadable stream at my feet and all the gentler water on the other side under the trees. Below me, the open island bank ran fifty yards or so down to a cluster of birch trees which I might, with difficulty, manage to pass, but they were succeeded by another clump and various bushes hanging out over the water. They were impassable. Down there, the pool speeded up and gathered force before entering the March Pool below. I was in a sticky position. The salmon was, by now, very tired, beginning to wallow well out on the other side of the stream and, when I could glimpse it in the darkness, seemed to be showing a tired tail. I turned on my hand lamp at one point to see what the fish was like and there it was lying immobile on the top of the stream, ready for the net if I had only had someone to do it, but absolutely out of my reach in that deep, unwadable water. Whenever I moved, the fish dropped back. As long as it had a spark of energy in it, I could let it get out of the stream on the far side and walk it up to safer places, but now it was virtually dead. It was just hanging there in the water, ready to be carried down by the heavy current if I released any pressure at all, and nowhere on the lower pool was within my possible reach. This was a kind of stalemate I have met several times in playing fish. The fish was fairly beaten and rod pressure could hold the tired fish at a certain point in a stream; to release pressure and approach it to net it would cause the fish to be washed downstream out of reach. There is really nothing one can do at all. This Dee fish wallowed a little as it lay exhausted, took line bit by bit through the force of the current, gained pace as the heavier stream caught it, and disappeared into the tail of the pool, where the hook-hold quietly gave.

I checked my flies and cast and as quickly as I could I went back to the head of the pool to see whether the sea trout were still rising, but it was virtually over. I pulled two, but the pulls were half-hearted. I had, after all, fought a lively salmon hard through the pool for forty minutes during the sea-trout rise. On a slower pool I would have waited and sunk my flies to search out a sea trout or two after the surface rise had ended, but on McKidd's Pool, with a fast, dark stream, this technique was unlikely to work. That salmon had, in a sense, robbed me of what looked like being a first-class hour of sea-trout sport. Had it been landed, it would have been some form of compensation and it would have been a kind of triumph to get one out of that particular pool on a single-handed rod. As it was, I made my long way back over the wade – or it seemed a long way in the dark. I had one two-pound seat trout for my night, despite almost constant contact and activity for two hours.

McKidd's Pool was formed by the Dee during a flood. Willie

McKidd died in the autumn of 1982 and shortly afterwards a great Dee flood took away McKidd's Pool. So the new head ghillie told me. I have not yet been able to get down to see the extent of the damage. They say the flood which ruined the pool opened up the March Pool again after years of being gravelled up. I hope it has. I see a kind of poetic act of the Dee in all this, taking McKidd's Pool away the winter he died. Let's hope the river, in its wisdom, after a decent interval, presents us with another pool there, because it is a wonderful place for night sea trout.

Salmon at night sometimes rise like sea trout. I mean, they rise with that marvellous plop to the night cast as it comes through a glide or searches out a runnel below a jetty. I do not know why most salmon go dead as darkness falls yet some may rise in the dark as if they were sea trout. I usually manage to cover one or two such fish in the course of a season when the salmon rise to me in places in which I expect a sea trout.

A typical fish pretending it was a sea trout came to my fly one July evening in the late seventies when I was fishing the Shiel. The seventies were poor for sea trout all over Scotland. Disease and, possibly, spawning failure contributed to their serious decline. The Shiel, which I had revelled in in the sixties, lost much of its stock, but when I was given the chance to go back and try it again on a July evening I went back full of optimism, with all the old feelings resurging, all the old experiences being relived and the highest of hopes. All the old places were there – Grassy, the Stages, the tail of Captain's – and each place produced a marvellous array of sensations. But what I actually found was a river which seemed to have reverted to salmon. I say that almost in a pejorative sense. The Shiel was such a splendid sea-trout river that it has always been difficult for me to think of it in any other bracket. Since then, the river has done its best to show me salmon of memorable quality and I am almost converted. But I still hope for a return to great sea-trout runs in June and early July.

I was fishing the Dorlin bank and the reach I had been given for the night was from Grassy down the stages. For those who have not seen the Shiel, I ought to explain 'stages'. From a very early date, the Shiel has had casting platforms, timber walkways and jetties constructed along its pools to make access and

99

fishing easier. The section below the great House Pool takes the river down through a narrow gorge with steep, heathery, well treed banks. Stages exist on both sides, but on the northern (Dorlin) bank they take the form of a series of little jetties angled out downstream into the river. Below each jetty there is a lie and in one of these I had a strong plopping rise to my sea-trout cast. I would have taken an oath that the rise came from a sea trout. I checked my flies and immediately covered the lie again. The time the same plop came and I was into the fish. The first thought that went through my head was 'Ah, so the Shiel still has heavy sea trout in it!' The fish had taken not far from the lie which had given me an 8½-pounder, followed by a six-pounder, followed by a five-pounder one fabulous night in the sixties. Old feelings convinced me that I was again into a good Shiel fish. My conviction that it was a sea trout blinded me to the obvious fact that the fish had not shown, had not run fast, had not leapt. Prejudiced mind over matter! Even in fishing, what *is* is sometimes subordinated to what might have been.

About halfway through the fight, I began to realise that this fish was not behaving like a sea trout. It returned to its lie and made one or two big circles. At this point I found myself hoping that the fish would turn out to be a big, rather sluggish sea trout. If it had in fact turned out to be a big seat trout, I would, of course, have forgiven it for being sluggish in the fight! Towards the end of the fight, when it was a slow solid sort of event, making my 9½-foot rod hoop well over as I applied pressure to the fish, I realised that it was a salmon whose nearest point of similarity to a sea trout had been the fast plopping rise. It was netted, weighed six and a half pounds, and was, really, a nice little fish. But I confess to feeling a little bit like Burns when he looked into a fashionable country house and saw the nobility dancing. Beautiful girls abounded, but they did not attract him that night. None of them was the girl he was in love with:

> *I sighed, and said amang them a',*
> *'Ye are na Mary Morrison.'*

Salmon at night sometimes interrupt good sea-trout fishing and they usually play much more sluggishly than sea trout. They also fight in a much more pedestrian way than they do by day – as if they are half asleep when you hook them. One or two exceptions have come my way. There was a particular fish on the Dee, on the splendid Quithel Pool on the Birse water one May night. I was at my usual trick of fishing salmon on the long rod until the light went and then changing to the sea-trout rod with a two-fly cast on and searching out the tails of the pools where sea trout gather in the dark. Being an opportunist, I tied a one-inch Stoat's Tail tube fly on the tail – a perfectly respectable choice for sea trout at night, but also a strong possibility for a salmon in the gloom. I suppose I was hedging my bets a little. Several salmon had been showing down near the tail of the Quithel but they had resolutely refused all my flies during the lighter part of the evening. It was now after eleven and, although it was night, it was the kind of night we get in Scotland on fine summer evenings. It was a white night. I could see the other bank, but it was as if it had been washed in grey watercolour. I waded in a little to reach what I thought was the right place for sea trout – the glide out of the pool which holds in to the far bank there. I case several times, moved down a bit and tried again, but although the conditions for sea trout seemed perfect I had no offers. I let my flies wash round below me to the very lip of the pool where the water begins to pick up for the wide head to the Trees run below and I had a vicious take. It was a take which turned into a run at once. I had no doubt at all that it was a salmon and a jolly lively one at that. I had to cope with two long, fast runs with leaps before I could get out of the water. I should explain that my estate car was parked on the grass near the tail of the pool, just behind me, and, knowing that I was into something larger than my sea-trout net would cope with easily, I conceived the idea of tiring the fish in the broad tail of the pool, then gently walking back to the car, opening the tailgate, and getting out my big Gye net, which would handle the salmon more easily. It was a great plan, don't you think? Unfortunately it did not work out exactly as I had thought. The fish had been extraordinarily lively and had made my reel make noises which raised it from a scream to a superscream during the runs. I thought the fish would have thoroughly winded itself in the process, and indeed things settled down to a period of pulsing and short runs and some rather more settled behaviour. I walked slowly backwards to the car and as I did so the fish shot off for the far bank with its afterburners going. If my reel had made screams before, it made falsetto noises now and seemed to be about to distintegrate. It was rather daft. I was walking one way and the salmon was going hell for leather in the other. But I have a cussed streak in me, or is it just stupidity? I was within reach of the tailgate of the Volvo, I was playing a fish from what seemed the middle of a pasture, but I was determined to get the big net. Up went the tailgate, out came the net. I retrieved line fast as I worked my way back to the river and, would you believe it, the fish was still on. This time it really was tired out and I netted it with a great sense of satisfaction. It was a superb fresh fish of ten pounds, and, unlike some of my night salmon, it was added to the bag with the greatest sense of achievement and satisfaction.

Taking salmon at night on the fly, as I have said, can sometimes be wonderful sport and can sometimes be quite dull. The largest salmon I have had in the dark was a 13½-pound fish from the Endrick, taken from Craigbell above Gartness. It took a size 8 Soldier Palmer on the dropper, pulled dourly and swam steadily round and round near its lie, never showing and never running. It had all the characteristics of a large wet sack. Indeed, I may do a disservice to sacks in saying so, because a friend of mine, asked what his best fight had ever been, said that his most memorable moment had been when he hooked a fertiliser bag at Waulkmill on the Tay when he was fishing fly. The bag opened out when he pulled and was taken downstream by the current, just like a fish. When he slacked off the bag collapsed and he was able to manoeuvre it upstream again, like a walked-up salmon. But my Endrick fish fought like a tired bag, not a sporting one. It was a nice fish, however, and looked well on the bank.

Sometimes salmon can be exceedingly tiresome at night when they rise to your fly and do not take it. This is particularly true of grilse and I describe one such experience on the Dee in Chapter 19. It really is extraordinary to fish a pool on a warm summer night – a pool you know is full of fish – and, in the dusk and dark, have salmon follow the fly, splash at it, boil at it, head-and-tail over it and produce not even the sensation of a touch. This usually happens when the river temperature is in the middle and upper sixties. Tepid nights for salmon! Perhaps the only way to make them move is to fish a very large fly, say a light Collie Dog a couple of inches long, or a lure with a long trailing hackle. Even then I have seen larger lures producing larger splashes and no proper takes.

It would clearly be misleading to say that salmon do not take at night. The preceding pages show that this cannot be true. Yet I take the view that salmon which take at night do so as a kind of aberration. I know how well salmon can take in the dusk as the light seeps out of the sky, but they change their behaviour as soon as the darkness comes. Great holding pools on the Dee and Spey, which are alive with crashing and boiling fish all day, fall into a short period of productive silence at dusk, when you have a high chance of taking a fish, and then into a period of dullness, with few or no fish showing. This marks the end of the salmon day for me. Sport will not start again until daybreak.

15

Salmon Among the Weeds

Anglers have a love–hate relationship with weeds. On the one hand weeds provide shelter, produce interesting stream variations, form holding lies in otherwise open pools, and in lochs mark shallows and fertile banks. In trout fishing they harbour and produce food in the form of myriads of nymphs, shrimp and snail. The negative side is that weed is a hazard. It catches flies which would otherwise fish well over lies, it prevents you sinking the cast and, above all, it presents a major hazard when you are playing fish. You know the feeling well. You are into a decent trout and all goes well for a couple of minutes. You are just beginning to think you might get the fish up over the weeds and into the net when the fish manages to dive head first into a trailing column of weed. The line goes dead, or nearly so. Somewhere inside the weed you are conscious of still being attached to the fish. There is the odd kick, and the resistance is

104

more solid than the weed itself would justify. Then the mass of weed begins to move under your steady rod pressure (or direct line pressure, if you are desperate) and you find a ball of weed moving slowly in. If you are lucky, inside it will be a very still trout. I don't know why trout are so still in weed. Perhaps they just can't move a muscle. If you are unlucky, you will find that all you have brought in is weed.

I recall killing a good fresh sea trout on Garrison on the Shiel. In certain pools the Shiel can be a spectacularly weedy river and both banks ring with stories of successes and losses in the weed. In my case, I was fishing at night and it was well on towards the next morning of the short summer darkness. It was that time of the night when there is a lull and I had switched to the sinking line to tempt the fish – a tactic which I find works well when there is little surface interest. On that June night it proved to be the right thing to do. I was working my way through the deep head of the pool when I had a fine pull from a fish and was into him. I got the line out of the water and felt reasonably secure and the fish fought largely on the top, leaping and splashing nicely. I could see its white form walloping around in the dark in the fairly open deep stream. But inside the main stream lay the hazard, a thick wall of trailing weed. I hoped to quieten the fish, then bring it over the top of the weed in a single steady pull. Well, not for the first time, I was wrong. The fish came easily at first, but as it approached the wall of weed it saw its last chance of escape and dived straight in like a missile. The line went dead and my heart sank. Instead of being attached to a lively fresh sea trout I was solidly into a mass of weed. I had a dropper on and that didn't make me feel any easier. My 8-pound cast was reasonably strong, but would it stand the direct strain of moving both fish and weed? Nothing seemed to be working so I lowered the rod top and pulled steadily. There was a moment of solid resistance, then I felt the weed coming away and I saw in the gloom a great mass of weed moving in towards me. I moved into the water and netted it and inside it was a splendid 3½-pound sea trout. There must have been half a sackful of weed in the net too.

It is interesting that, althouth one hears of large trout, wise in the ways of escape, making for weeds as soon as they are hooked, it is my experience that sea trout and salmon, and particularly the latter, keep well clear of the weeds during the earlier part of the fight and only push their noses in when they are tired, usually when you are bringing the fish in to shallow water prior to netting. Clearly, weed means at least two things to a fish like a salmon. It represents shelter from stream and from view, but in my view it also represents something slightly insidious, something unknown, something to be shunned in normal times. On weedy rivers, there is no doubt at all that salmon lie well in weedy pools, particularly those pools with a good stream which have trailing columns of weed forming corridors. On rivers like the Shiel – but similarly in many West Highland waters and in weedy sections of the middle and lower Tweed – some of your best lies are among weed.

I remember one such pool on the Shiel, the Blacksmith's, which is so weedy that you can't easily wade out into it. At certain times of the summer, particularly August and early September, fish lie well there and can usually be seen head-and-tailing, or rising like trout in the late evening. It is tremendous fishing to put a small hair-wing fly over them. By day you need a wind on the pool, but as the light goes, if you are careful, you can rise and hook fish as dusk falls. I had failed to do well one evening and, having access to the pool the next morning, got up from breakfast and buzzed off to try the fish in daylight. The daylight showed just how extensive the weeding was. The pool was virtually closed except for the channels I have mentioned, and the thick columns of weed were waving and snaking like great eel-like monsters. Out in the middle a fish showed, just a nose and a tail. I waded in as far as I had to and found myself in a corridor, casting a fairly long line over the weed to let the fly fish the lies in the middle and near the left bank opposite. There was one boil, but it came to nothing. Then I popped the fly over again and this time, without much surface indication, I had the slight stop and the pull and was into him. My fear was that the fish would weed me at once but, as I have said, few fish do. The fish rapidly moved up and down the corridors in the middle of the pool, and I was able to keep my rod high and let the line follow the fish safely. It was not a big fish, seven pounds or so, typical of the West Highland summer runs. It tired itself out among the weeds, put up a weary tail, and then a back, and I was able to pull the fish over the intervening walls of weed and into my own corridor where, with only a frond or two of weed, I netted him. I stopped fishing and went back to the house I was staying in, where my host was still getting ready for the river, and declared the first fish of the day.

I don't think I have ever lost a salmon during the fight in a trailing column of weed. I have had some large fish in the upper teens crashing about in weedy pools in the Highlands and although I have lost some of them I have not lost them because they went into weed. I have netted fish covered in weed, but that has mostly been picked up as the fish has been steered in through the shallows.

There is one particularly hazardous stream on the Tweed, the Gatesheugh, on the upper part of Bemersyde, where weed helps to hold fish, and causes two odious hazards for the angler. Not only does the Gatesheugh weed sometimes lose you a fish, it makes wading dangerous. The Gatesheugh is an infuriating stream. It follows a long, rocky and shingly course, hard in to the right bank of the Tweed. The Bemersyde rod has to wade out, following a long and wearisome route through weed, up and down over rock ledges and boulders, and then at last on to the ridge, which you can fish down, covering lovely streamy holding water, down to the odd part of the stream they call the Dish. That is a magnificent place to fish fly, but like all glory it has to be struggled for and sometimes paid for. The Dish fishes best when the river is a few inches up. If it is too many inches up, you will have a struggle to reach it – and there hangs many a tale. The ghillie at Bermersyde says he is going to have a medal struck to be presented to all those who can take a fish off the Gatesheugh or the Dish and not fall in. The wading hazard of weeds is awkward, at its lowest, and at its highest can be dangerous. Weed tends to form what I have called corridors and these sometimes mark out the ridges on the pool bottom. If you wade down ridges, as we do on such streams as the Gatesheugh on Tweed, you can find yourself moving downstream fairly easily, but, at critical points, having to cross from one ridge to the other. If the intervening water is shallow enough, this is awkward, but possible. Columns of weed trailing downstream produce barriers and these can be anything from tedious to alarming. I hate the feeling of weed wrapping itself round my waders. Of course, weed round the legs can be shaken or torn off in most cases without too much trouble. But the effort of doing it is wearing and the movements can make you lose your footing.

If you are obliged to inch your way back upstream, trailing weed can be very difficult. You are pushing back up into the hanging weed, parting the fronds, and moving in towards its roots on the boulders or on the bottom upstream of you. This can make you alter route off the ridges and into deeper water. The very fact that you are making your way back upstream indicates that you have run into water too deep for comfort below you. Having to divert on the route to safety can be just the movement which will upset you and earn you half the medal I mentioned.

It can be curious playing fish so far out over the Tweed in water varying from thigh-deep to waist-deep and in bottom conditions consisting of downstream ridges, boulders and lots of weed. I remember a November fish I took there. It fought well in the Dish among the weeds and, like most salmon, kept itself clear of the weeds in the process. I decided to walk it straight in, and I was fairly certain of my route at that height of water. I crossed the ridges with their weeds and the salmon followed compliantly. Halfway in it suddenly woke up and thought it ought to go back out to the main stream again. I managed to dissuade it and the fish then began to circle me in the weedy shallowing water I was now in. It was curious to turn like a top and follow the fish round. There is no particular hazard in this, provided you do not have any line lying in the water, say after handlining in. But who would handline for any reason at that stage in the fight? Watch your net; it can get fouled up and you are just about to use it. This circling is the tactic of a weak fish and its normal equivalent is the circling a fish usually does just before turning over and being led to the net. I was reminded on that occasion, as the salmon circled me, of the many times this happens to me in the dark when I am playing sea trout on the Spey. There, the difficulty is knowing which way the fish has run round you. I have found myself straining to see the rod top against the gloom of the night sky so that I might turn in the right direction. No, I do not have a theory that fish turn clockwise in the northern hemisphere and anti-clockwise in the southern, like bathwater draining out! Spey sea trout go one way or the other as the fight defines itself. Fish will start one way and suddenly turn and dash back to circle in the other direction. Salmon, as usual, are simpler fish to play and circling is much more sedate.

I netted my Tweed fish, waded slowly to the bank with it well bagged in the Gye net and knocked it on the head. Some of my friends think you should kill such fish in the net. I think this is far too hazardous, although I sometimes do this at night when I am fishing sea trout. But they are easier. You can hold a sea trout in one hand, using the net as a grip, and with a handy priest, say one hung round your neck, you can kill the fish and transfer it to a polythene bag strung round your neck, or slide it into a bag on your back, or, as I do, slide it into a washable poacher's pocket in my Barbour jacket. I do not think it is safe to tuck your rod under your arm, grapple with a fair-sized salmon bagged in the net, kill it, and then wade ashore. If you have the fish bagged and if you are wading ashore anyway, the fish is relatively safe. Don't choose that moment to fall in, however. As a kind of insurance, if your net is large enough (and it should be), once the salmon is bagged, turn the ring over and as it were lock the fish in the bag of the net. This will hold it effectively and you have a fair chance of saving the fish even if you do stumble and ship water as you wade in.

Weeds – friend and foe – help enormously in lochs. There are some summer salmon lochs which seem to be more weed than water, and that can be a problem, but even in these cases salmon lies can be pinpointed by reference to bays in the weeds and similar features. In larger lochs, like Maree, the appearance of weeds at or near the surface often marks out the area of shallow water in which salmon like to lie. Without these weed markers, it would be difficult to find some of the open-water lies on lochs. Salmon are shallow-water fish in lochs. Weeds mark out the shallows. In strange lochs, fish over the weeds and you will not go far wrong. In well-known lochs weeds known to you single out the lies and make your fishing accurate.

I have been lucky enough to have had some fabulous summer salmon fishing in weedy pools. On one long glide thick with columns of weeds, where a river leaves a large Highland loch, a friend and I took eleven fish in two sessions – an afternoon and the following morning. The weeds not only held the fish well but shielded us from the salmon, and in some measure kept the struggles of one fish from affecting the lies we had not so far covered. We kept our heads down, and used eleven-foot rods with small black flies (it didn't seem to matter which pattern, as long as it was small and black) and the fish came well. Twice during that interesting morning my colleague and I found ourselves playing fish at the same time. We landed the first two, but I lost mine the second time it happened. Who says lightning does not strike twice in the same place? In salmon fishing, a success is often instantly replayed, because conditions are right.

Weeds have now come to mean salmon to me on West Highland rivers in summer and my heart leaps up when I look into such pools as Piper's on the Shiel, or the astonishing Cliff Pool which has a couple of hundred yards of weedy glide ending in a fine weedy pot from which, one June day, I took my best couple of summer fish ever, eighteen and a half and sixteen and a half pounds, shining fresh from the sea and as wild as tigers. These fish were taken from lies among weeds. Any one of them could have broken me in an instant by diving into weed columns, but no salmon or sea trout has yet done this to me. On balance, then, it seems to me that weeds are far more often friends than foes in salmon fishing, even if they threaten disaster on occasion.

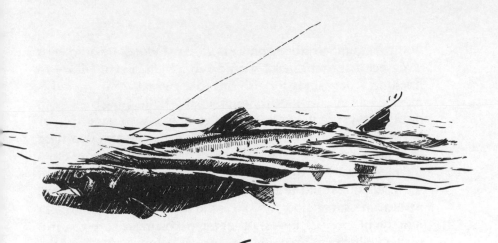

16

Hooking Salmon on the Fly

Salmon can, sometimes, be amazingly co-operative when it comes to taking a fly well and getting well hooked. Every one of us has had the experience of feeling the pull of a taking salmon, raising the rod in our normal way, playing the fish, and finding – despite anxieties during the fight – that when the fish comes to the net it has engulfed the fly, hooked itself well back in the mouth, and would not have freed itself in a month of Sundays. But haven't many of us had the same scenario – the solid take, the slow, seemingly effective tightening and the hook falling out during the fight, or, if you are lucky, falling out in the net.

What factors affect hooking salmon well on fly? After a season when I carried out several experiments in my own fishing I have come to some conclusions.

Over many salmon-fishing years, the last six of which have been devoted to fly-fishing exclusively, I find that I have become a particular kind of fisher; I 'give him line and scope'. I hate

111

pulling a salmon directly on a short line. Indeed, I would lay a large bet that such a take would run a high risk of failure in hooking. I like fishing longish lines for salmon, even when this means that I must artificially lengthen line by keeping back from the lies. Now, that is not Irish. The line is a splendid buffer between you and the fish, provided it is handled well. A tight line, no matter how long, is disaster for salmon fishing. On a tight line, say a line running directly down a low rod pointing at the fish, you would feel the pull as a heavy, sudden tug and would almost certainly not hook the fish, or at best get a light hold on his nose. If, on the other hand, you make sure you fish with a high rod point, keeping a droop between the tip of the rod and the fly, you have a high chance of hooking the fish well.

This idea of giving line and scope is an absolutely essential principle in salmon fly-fishing, but there are many ways of achieving this end. Perhaps the most straightforward technique is, quite simply, keeping one's rod tip up. This approach – which I call *creating droop* – is particularly useful on streamy water where pulls can be sudden and fierce, since fish move faster in a stream than they do in slower water. Further, in a stream you cannot always see the fish moving, and the pull is the first indication of a take.

On Tweed and on some of the other larger salmon waters of Scotland, numbers of anglers use a combination of creating droop and giving line. Line is held in a large loop between the reel and the index finger of the right hand on the rod handle. The theory of this double safety measure is that the angler can release the loop – usually about two yards or so – as the pull is felt, allowing the fish to turn and hook itself solidly. It often does. What usually goes wrong with this approach is that anglers are startled by the pull and react to it not by releasing the loop of line but by involuntarily gripping the line tighter to the butt and thus putting strain on the fish far too soon, often with the result that fish are hooked forward on the mouth or not at all.

I have fished this way for many years, whether with floating or sunk line, and I have had some good results in hooking. But I have to admit that it is only recently, after over thirty years of salmon fishing, that I have felt cool enough about takes to let the fish take line through my fingers as it turns. But, cool or not, I strongly recommend anglers to build in droop as well as loop to

their line handling to give some form of insurance against tightening too soon.

In 1982, at the beginning of a fabulous day's fishing on middle Tweed in early autumn, I switched to a hooking technique which I had occasionally used with effect in the past – striking off the reel. I found on one astonishing day in late September that I hooked two fish well right at the beginning of the morning by using the droop and loop approach, but I was astonished to note how slow the draws were before I felt that it was time to raise the rod and pull the hook home. I was, as usual, fishing a slow-sinking No. 10 line on a fifteen-foot 'Yorkshire' carbon fly rod and, while I was very far from dredging as I fished, my 1¾-inch Brora Waddington with its size 8 treble was fishing fairly well down into the water and was liable to being taken in a sideways take, rather than an up-and-down take.

This last point is important, I feel. When we are fishing floating line the salmon rises to the fly, perhaps coming up through three or four feet of water to it, possibly breaking the surface as it takes. You know the kind of take I am referring to. The fish suddenly appears and seems to nod quite quickly at the fly. You have your rod held up with created droop and, as the fish turns down, the droop allows it scope and inside a couple of seconds you are tightening into the fish and getting the hook well home. In sunk-line fishing the presentation of the fly is radically different. It is well out of sight. Its depth is not so much a function of the weight of the fly (in my case certainly not) as a product of the line being well settled in the water as it fishes round. I like the word 'settled' rather than 'sunk' to give the right distinction between what happens with a slow-sinking line and what would happen with a fast sinker. Indeed, to continue the aside, I confidently believe that the fly on a slow-sinking line rides up above the line on many occasions and takes fish above the level of settlement of the line itself.

Fish taking a sunk fly, in spring or in autumn, are presented with the fly near their lying depth, and take by turning sideways on the fly as it hovers or swims past. In streamy water particularly these takes can give the longest, slowest draws imaginable. They test the nerve and they astonish many an experienced rod. That autumn day, it was the suggestion of a young, keen ghillie which brought this again to my attention.

'They're taking very slowly,' I observed. 'Why not strike them off the real?' he replied.

Striking off the reel can only really be carried out if you are fishing practically the whole cast round without handlining. This is typical of the Tweed full of water, with plenty of life in the pools and glides you are likely to be fishing. It is also going to be typical of fishing a slow-sink line which does not dredge, but which settles and fishes itself round at the speed allowed by the stream. It takes some nerve at first to leave the line completely free of your hands, and running straight off the reel. To match the conditions you are faced with, you can either fish a modestly high top or, as I like doing, fish a low top, virtually pointing the rod at where the salmon is likely to take. The take itself is electrifying. You feel the pull before the reel speaks. There is a sudden twitch of the line at the rod top, and the message through the rod that a fish has taken. Then the reel speaks. Sometimes it is a slow beginning, a long steady buzz of the ratchet, speeding up suddenly as the fish seems to turn viciously on the fly and, like a dog pulling a scarf, giving it a sudden hard, twisting pull. You tighten into the fish only when this has happened. To stop this process early will seriously imperil the hooking. Sometimes, I would say most times, the take is faster and much more sudden. The reel bursts into life, giving a long, high scream. Again, the important thing is to *let the fish take line from the reel*. What is actually happening is that the fish has turned on the fly, takes it with him in a downstream turn, perhaps giving it a good twisting tug as it goes, and then turns into its lie again. You hook the fish when the reel stops, or – I will concede this – just as it is about to stop.

I had the good luck to take fifteen fish in two days early in October in 1982, and again, when the waters settled on the Tweed at the end of November, I had the incredible jammy luck to take seventeen salmon in the last two days of the season. Let me say at once that I do not normally take vast bags of salmon like this. My previous best was eight in a day, and it is many years since it happened. Fours and fives are not unusual in autumn on the Tweed and in the fabulous spring of 1978 I had six springers one day on fly in the Dee. My catches are really like anybody else's. I have long blanks, some steady days of a fish or two for my labours, some lucky days of a few more, and, a couple of times in my very full fishing life – and they both happened in the autumn of 1982 – a bounty of salmon, and a feeling almost of shame because the sport was so concentrated.

I believe that hooking fish off the reel in the Tweed in Autumn, and in spring fishing pretty well everywhere, where a slow-sink line is involved, is far more effective than any other method I have used. It is very thrilling, gives big fish time to turn, lets the fly go well back in the mouth, and maximises your chances of a good hold.

I have in the past had super sport on the Dee, fishing in this way with floating line and a size 6 double. I have had wonderful sport on my sea-trout rod with small summer salmon on the west coast of Scotland, again letting the fish make the reel speak. One the negative side, I have, time and again, lost fish which I tightened on far too soon. Striking from the reel, where it can be done, is excellent fishing. Alas, it cannot easily be combined with any tactic where variable handlining is involved. There, as you gather line in and actively fish the fly – as in most floating-line fishing – you must give the fish line and scope by the tactic of creating droop and releasing loop to give it time to take well.

115

17

Nooks and Crannies

In one of our moods, we are prone to reconstruct past fishing on Highland rivers in terms of great straths, sweeps of river swinging through heather and shingle and reaches of gorge, waterfall or rapids. In another mood, equally satisfying, what we recall can be highly detailed, very clearly focused corners where salmon have been seen, risen and, with luck, taken. It is almost a case of the microscope rather than the telescope. I am very much a nooks and crannies fisher, especially on difficult days, and it seems to me that the fish I take from odd little places on rivers etch themselves deeply in the mind.

In one sense, every salmon is a fish of a nook or cranny. Salmon inhabit lies, quite clearly defined places in the streams and pools of the river. When you fish down a great sweep of

116

a pool, like the Lummels on the Dee at Aboyne, or like the Junction Pool on the Tweed at Kelso, what you are conscious of is the pool. You know that somewhere in the stream fish find the kind of shelter they want and when you are 'pool-minded' you fish for them by covering the whole stream consistently. When fish take you, you are not sure what lie they have risen from. Is there a boulder on the bed, or a hollow in the shingle, or a ledge of rock to form the lie? When you fish the nooks and crannies of a river you go into a different gear and specifically fish tiny areas of water sometimes right under your rod top. It demands a different approach but taking fish from these places produces the greatest fishing satisfaction.

I was fishing the Lochy in September with a good water running. Bully for him, I hear you say. In fact it was very far from bully. I was on beat 3 and the glides and pools of Camisky had produced nothing whatever for three rods up to lunch time. Fishing a hopeless river with low water and getting nothing is one thing, but to find the Lochy with three feet of flood in it and dropping and still getting nothing from pools with reputations which are second to none in Scotland brings on a special kind of anxiety. I remember lunch that day being decidedly pianissimo. The stories were a little attenuated. *Angst* had gripped us all.

I was sent first to fish the tail of the pool above the falls, and the water looked superb. It was just too high to wade effectively and get the angle on the fly I wanted. Reaching a lie is one thing, but fishing it is another. I saw a couple of red fish splashing in the eddy on the far side, unreachable. I saw what I thought was a fresh fish showing where salmon normally show after running the falls, and I had the sinking feeling that by the time I covered the lie the fish might have been a hundred yards upstream, running hard. We knew that the whole gorge below the falls was out of ply since there was too much water and it was suggested that I should go to the turbulent Fence Pool below the gorge and try a fly there.

I should explain that the Fence Pool is also the ferrying place where anglers are taken over to the right bank to walk down to the beautiful Garden Pool below. I stook looking at the water, dark and turbulent and rather angry in the flood. Above the pool lay the maelstrom of the gorge and the roaring of the falls. I cast my fly, a one-inch Willie Gunn, over the tail of the pool where

the turbulent water suddenly recovered its sense of direction and fanned out to disperse to deep, slow water on my left, and to form the main stream to the right of a large shingle bank below me. Over on the far side were several large rocks and beyond them a deepish rocky stream hard under the trees where the water divided to form a series of most attractive small glides. I could not reach these rocks from my left bank. Wading was out of the question, with rock ledges plunging down to who knows what black depths on my side. As you might expect, a salmon showed just above the three rocks near the other bank, absolutely unfishable from my left-bank stand.

The rod on the far bank came back up the path. I could tell by his step that the Garden Pool had not produced a fish. I called across, making gestures like the silent movies to say that I had seen a fish above the rocks and that they should try to cover it as they came across in the boat. They did, but the boat swung and screwed round in the turbulence, covering the fish was extremely difficult, and it was left. My hunting instinct was up. I was absolutely certain that fish were lying in the area immediately above the cluster of rocks, perhaps unfishable, and were surely in the nice divided streams within and around the rocks. Could the boat not be held for a few seconds at least to let me pop a fly into the lie I saw on the near side of the big rock and in the tantalising little glide within the cluster?

The young ghillie thought that perhaps it could, and I embarked. I have sat in one or two difficult boats in my time, but that was a pig of a row for the ghillie. You could not tell where the next upsurge would hit the boat and where it would take it. This meant that I had to lengthen and shorten line, change direction of cast and fish the fly somehow in a relatively steady way over the two small lies. About one cast in three landed right and made some semblance of fishing properly. Hard beside the large boulder on the glide on my side I had a fast, clear take and was into a fish which immediately left the lie and headed for the still water below. I was taken ashore to play it, but a couple of minutes after I got the hooks in the little Willie Gunn came out. This is always a problem with fast, restricted lies. The fish snatches at the fly and is at best lip-hooked. I was desperately sorry to lose that fish. It had all the qualities of a fish into the teens of pounds.

We went in again and fished the same lie and again I had a take in almost the same spot. Again I was landed and again the little treble hook came out. Disaster! Two takes on a blank day and two losses. Misery on wheels. I thought I had better change my fly and try something with a larger treble and a size 6 Drury Stoat's Tail caught my eye. On it went and after some manoeuvres I managed to plop it accurately inside the rock crown into the attractive small divided stream it carried. This time the take felt different. I felt the fish, gave it time, and raised the rod to contact a small fish apparently firmly hooked. I was again landed and this time had no problems. It was only six pounds, but on that blank day was a most welcome salmon. It was, like the two I had lost, a salmon from a tiny nook, an almost inaccessible place among stones, and that made it worth twice its weight.

Nooks are sometimes as small as a bathroom mirror. In turbulent water they show up as sudden glassy patches, which are the surface hint that there is respite from the stream below the surface. For instance, we were having lunch on beat 6 of the Helmsdale, just below the Kildonan Falls. The river that early March day was running high and the falls were impressive. The Falls Pool was unfishable, and the fast streams below were absolutely out. The fish we had been getting that day came from the Vale of Tears, just below the gorge, and the Manse well below that at the next corner. As we came off for lunch I said to the ghillie that there was one little patch of the Falls Pool over on the far side where a tiny burn came in which looked glassy and might just fish. It was an area about half the size of a bathtub, glassy and looking privileged in an area of fast, broken water.

I sat having lunch and thinking about it until I could wait no longer. I left my sandwiches and my glass of wine, lifted my rod, and went to the side of the Falls Pool. I tied on a two-inch Brora fly, a black and orange, lengthened line and managed to plop the fly into the glassy patch. Up he came, like a trout, taking the big fly firmly and well, and I was into him. The fight was difficult, because I had to bring the fish over the fast water of the tail of the Falls Pool and if it had taken the notion to go down with the flood it would go through fast, rocky water in which there was every chance of a break. But the fish fought most of the time in the tail of the pool itself, tiring in due course against the hard

119

stream, and at length I managed to get the salmon in. George Hardy, the ghillie, who had been keeping an eye on my rod top from the lunch spot, ran down with the net and had him out neatly. It was a lovely fresh fish from a very restricted lie in a pool which was unfishable in the conventional sense.

A good ghillie will show you the nooks and crannies on a pool. Some are hardly visible to a stranger. Yet you can develop a good eye for likely water. A likely place for a productive nook is hard beside the fast headstream of a pool – the neck. Running fish lie there, often in very restricted areas, waiting for the moment to run the fast water above. On the Helmsdale on lower beat 5 beside the headstream of the Breakwater Pool there is a splendid lie in the neck which has produced springers for me. It is difficult to fish, because you are fishing the big fly in from a fast stream and it sinks in the sheltered water of the lie itself unless you are particularly careful to keep your rod up and help the fly by handlining. The takes there are hard to deal with. A fish taking a handlined fly does not always give you any feel of a pull and you could very easily take the fly out of his mouth. The best lie, then, is covered on the dangle and even in good streamy water this is hard hooking, but on a slack lie where your fly sinks easily it is extraordinarily awkward at times. I say I have had fish there, but I ought also to say that I have had some spectacular misses there. I had a fine pull which I managed to bungle by taking the fly away and the ghillie commented that I had missed a springer. I thought so too, but the little lie suddenly opened and a great dark kelt sprang into the air. I suggested that I had perhaps missed that, but the ghillie was having none of it. He assured me, with the authority of a man who knows, that I had missed a springer and there might well be a kelt in the lie too. I didn't win in fishing terms, and in the short debate which followed I came off second best too.

It is interesting that above that lie in the Breakwater there is a pool called the Ewe's Neuk. In that case however, 'neuk' refers to a place on the sandy bank where the ewes shelter in bad weather. The stream you fish is an open piece of water in no way typified by nooks or crannies.

Running fish are often the salmon you take from these sheltered corners, and usually they fish best in a flood. I am not among those anglers who believe that you can catch running fish. I believe you can catch them when they stop, and they may do so for very small periods during their passage through a pool. In some cases I have seen a fish enter a pool and glide into the first sheltered lie near the tail. I have then quickly put the fly over the fish and have had him take. I suppose you could say that a fish resting for a minute or two in a lie and then going on upstream is a runner. I suppose he is, but while he is moving upstream I do not think he will take you. I love fishing when salmon are running, but I do not expect to take the fish as they move through the pool. When they stop, they often do so behind a stone or beside a stream or in a sheltered bay of the bank. These places are often hard to fish. They lie, typically, in fast water, where they provide shelter. If you can get into the water well above the lie and let your fly come round behind the stone, say, with a high rod top for insurance against sudden snatches, you have a chance of doing more than feel the pull. I do not feel secure fishing such places with very short lines. Some of them lend themselves to this approach, especially lies under the bank in floods. If you can fish a short line, rise your fish and hook him well you are expert. I much prefer to stand well back from the lie and let the line sweep the fly in. When the fish takes I have slack to take up his pull and turn. You can sometimes let the fish take line off the reel in the hooking process and this works well, as I described in the previous chapter. I am never happy to be too close on top of a fish in a nook.

On beats which you get to know intimately, wading them in low water and seeing exactly the configuration of the bed, it becomes clear that, as I said earlier, all salmon lie in nooks and crannies. In a way, it helps to know a river bed like this. There is no doubt that you can steer the fly round and make it hover productively over likely places. One of the interesting things about salmon in nooks, however, is that it is usually in floods that nooks come into their own, and in high water the nooks may be part of the path you usually walk down. As a river rises, it alters the whole pattern of lies, or rather lie-able lies. This is caused partly by the straightforward physical power of the risen river, but partly it is the result of different standing waves being formed on the bed. The theory of standing waves has had some prominence in recent years because it was made the basis of developing a new type of salmon pass. Salmon use the standing waves to leap, it was argued, and there seems to be clear evidence that this is true. But the same standing waves leave certain places on the bed of a stream comparatively sheltered. In these places, in invisible nooks sheltered from the pressure of the water, salmon lie. You will now expect me to pull something out of the hat and tell you how to fish such places. Alas, I do not know how to. These lies are under fast streams. All but a pure lead fly would be swept away before it fished there. I dare say past generations of salmon fishers might have managed to worm such lies, although I fancy they would, in high water, be productively employed in drowning worms in far more likely places, such as the sheltered nooks down the bank.

━ 18 ━
Sometimes Salmon Go Mad

The really gripping thing about salmon fishing is its uncertainty. The fish are migratory and we await their arrival with all manner of intensity, often with a rather painful anxiety. When the fish do arrive, forging up the streams and leaping tantalisingly in the tails of the pools, a special kind of fervour grips us. We reassure each other, rod to rod and ghillie to guest – 'We're in with a chance now. If they would just stop they would take you' or 'Fresh fish take pretty well anything, even your old fishing hat if you attach it to your line and cast it out.' There is a good measure of truth in both remarks. Fresh salmon, if they are not in that agitated state they get into when they are running fast upstream, are very likely chances for the angler. If the running fish stops, even to catch its breath, as it were, it is the most likely taker. On rivers like the Helmsdale and the Shiel, I have rapidly reeled in and have run down the bank to cover fish showing in a holding lie when the run was on. Why run? Because the fish which has arrived may only spend half a minute in the lie, before running further. The fish is uncatchable while it is running, but during its 'breather' is almost a certainty. I run in my chest waders for a strictly limited number of things. I run with the net to help a rod in distress when a salmon is proving difficult; I run when I absolutely have to follow a big fish fast downstream; and I run to cover a certain kind of holding lie, usually in spring, when a fish announces that it has stopped there.

When the fish settle in the pools of the river, they retain their *joie de vivre* for a few days and they are definitely temptable with the fly and, indeed, are often highly probable takers. But the abandon of the fresh fish, its sea spirit, wears off and what is left for us is a fish which comes on to the take from time to time, and scorns our best flies in between times.

When fish take is a mystery, although experience and a touch of science can help to reduce the chances loaded against us. Why fish take is a rather interesting area for speculation and the shelves of most anglers carry books and chapters in books on how it might be explained. Even in this book, I have said something about why fish take, but it will not take a genius to see that I am pleasing myself in my explanation, rationalising a curious phenomenon. There is not much in the way of scientific proof. I am not apologising for not being fully scientific about when and why salmon take, however. When we are honest about what we know about nature, we would all say that our knowledge is far more often in the realm of effective explanation than in definitive insight of how things work. We think as our culture has shaped us; we reduce the manifold of our experience to reason. When we have done that to the best of our ability, using the approaches and the techniques of explanation of our time, we have little more than a handhold on nature. I sometimes wonder whether we have even that in our explanation of salmon behaviour.

When salmon go slightly mad, I think we are very conscious that we don't know much about the fish at all, even if we can exploit the mad moments and catch fish. Let me give an example. Salmon are usually difficult to tempt, outside the free-rising period when they are fresh from the sea. Yet I have seen fish apparently trying to leave the river in their attempt to

124

take a fly swung over their stream. I have never actually seen a fish beaching itself in the attempt to take a fly drawn out of the water, but I have seen them in very shallow water and in difficulties as they follow the fly in. That is a nice little piece of madness. Much more commonly, I have seen salmon which, on taking the fly or bait, immediately swim up out of the river with it. I had a nice small May fish on the Tay once at Burnbane which took a Devon and immediately swam straight towards me and beached itself high and dry on the shingle at my feet. Once or twice I have had fish which have run straight out from me, early in the fight, and have stranded themselves on the shingle opposite. I know foul-hooked salmon will do this, but the fish I am referring to were properly hooked in the mouth. Sea trout do it, usually in a wild dash in which they may have lost their sense of direction. I have had trout and sea trout take the fly and immediately leap into the boat. This is easier to explain. I suspect they do not know the boat is there and they are merely leaping after being hooked. The phenomenon of salmon running up out of the river, however, is quite extraordinary, because they are very familiar with the confines of the pool or stream they have been lying in.

I have written before about salmon taking the fly madly after periods of dourness or just normal difficulty. In a book I wrote in the sixties, *A Gamefisher's Year*, I recorded an event I witnessed on the Thurso on that lovely beat just below Loch More where the stone bridge crosses the river. One April evening, fish began to rise like trout and I was able to take several before the peculiar rise went off. A local chap who appeared on the bridge told me of his extraordinary experience on that same pool on a previous evening. The pool had erupted with salmon rising like trout, making little rings on the surface and going mad over a dapped fly, as the local called it. In fact he was describing a form of dibbling, where a dropper, usually larger than the tail fly on the cast, is dapped and skated on the surface of the stream and salmon can go wild over it. In this case, however, the place he had taken the fish from was not a dibbling stream, but a virtually glassy pool with a glide out of it. The salmon came in that witching hour as the light dies and the wind goes down with it. He had taken eight fish one after the other during this period of madness. 'They took the gee,' he said. I

125

have never heard the word before but my Jamieson's *Scots Dictionary* soon filled me in on that count. It is an old Scots word meaning moodiness or madness. Many of the examples cited were about the behaviour of women. Jamieson and his sources were clearly not afraid of that form of chauvinism. He went on to cite poets who were said to 'tak the gee' when their verses contained wild conceits. Lovers were advised by some of Jamieson's citations not to let the gees of their lassies worry them too much. It has always made me chuckle that the unknown stranger on that bridge on the Thurso in 1965 should have used a word to describe the madness of the salmon which is usually reserved for whimsical behaviour in poets and women. I said at the time that this kind of salmon madness has a grain of the micraculous in it. I have not seen a gee like this since then, although I have seen wild rises. This special form of madness is obviously in short supply.

Wild behaviour of individual salmon is quite often met with. A few days before writing this chapter in February 1984 I had an encounter with a fish on the Helmsdale which was quite unusual. As you might imagine, February fishing up north begins with a small but very welcome number of fresh fish and a scattering of kelts. Now, I don't know what your experience is of fresh salmon in early spring. Mine is that they tend to take slowly and often quite softly. Indeed, one of the marks of pulling a fresh salmon as opposed to a kelt is that the fresh fish gives you a nice slow pull, or a couple of twitches and a pull as if the fish were quite deliberately mouthing the fly for the best hold. Kelts often pluck at the fly and in some cases do so weakly and fitfully, for the very good reason that they are just shadows of salmon after their spawning exertions of the previous winter. I was, on that occasion, fishing down the Tail of the Bay on lower beat 3, a fine glide with even pace draining a long moorland pool above where kelts are common. I was fishing from the right bank and I had a good line out, coming round slowly and carefully over the lies in mid-river, when I had perhaps the most violent take I have had in some forty years of salmon fishing. It was not a pull, it was a violent attack on the fly, and from the power of it I can only conclude that the fish turned on the fly and took it full pelt downstream. It did not stop, but snatched line and roared off in a run which would have graced any of Zane Grey's tarpons. At

126

the end of it, with all manner of backing off the reel, a substantial fine-looking fish leapt high out of the water, perhaps three or four feet, and cart-wheeled violently. Nor did it stop then, for the fish immediately tore across stream, drowning my line and causing me all sorts of anxiety. I had to reel in like mad, walk backwards briskly and do my best to keep in touch with this magnificent fish, which again leapt high and walloped into the water far down my bank. I got on terms with the fish after that and soon had him pulsing rather quietly under my rod just out from the bank. Off came the net and up came the fish for a final turn. I could not believe my eyes. It was a big fish, but it looked at me as I drew it in with that squint which characterises a kelt. I netted it, and took it ashore and quickly checked its gills. There were maggots in them. The vent was extruded and, although the fish was in excellent physical condition, with a good silver body with big scales, looking like a fine winter-run fish, it was clearly a kelt. I was at once astonished and disappointed. What a take! What a fight! What a disappointment! That mad kelt could have broken me had I not been fishing off the reel. It could have thrown the hook and I would have entered it into my list of heavy fish lost, assuming it to be a springer. At no time did I suspect that it was a kelt until the fish looked sideways at me as I drew it into the net.

Every angler has his stories of extraordinary salmon behaviour, often with happy endings as unusual fish are grassed. I have had two salmon on at once on a two-fly sea-trout cast. Fortunately I lost one, because my nine foot six cane rod would not have handled two to the net and, further, it was in the sea pool of the Shiel and the fish which was left attached did what many salmon there do – it ran fast downstream, over the first fall, into the pot below, over the second fall and down through the seaweedy stream into the tide itself. I had to follow and I netted the fish among the bladder wrack after a great chase. I have had two fish come for the same fly and, as one visibly took the fly, the other barged in and gave the first fish the shoulder and knocked it off. I did not see this well, since I was down there fishing with the line out over the head of the stream and fishing in the excellent lie which was produced on the other side. The ghillie was standing on the whinny bank above the fish and saw it clearly. He came quickly down and said, 'Did you see that?

127

Two salmon came at once and one knocked the other off!' For me, it was just a pluck and a rather strange commotion in the lie I was fishing.

Madness is often partly explained by aggression among fish as they jostle for the best redd or for proximity to the hen salmon. We are all fairly familiar with the stories of aggressive red cock fish in autumn whamming at the fly and showing all the characteristics of angry takes as opposed to the feeding takes which are typical of most salmon during the year. It is fairly unusual, however, to find hen fish being unusually aggressive. Yet, fishing late one September, I had a rather embarrassing if fascinating experience of fishing down a clear gravelly stream and having a whole succession of hen fish attack the fly, several of them being foul-hooked as a result. I had to leave the pool eventually. What was happening was that the fly was coming round and fish would leave the gravel, where, presumably they intended to cut redds in due course, and would swipe at the fly with their tails. The surface of the stream was boiling with this activity and at first I thought I had hit a wild taking moment. Quite frankly, I expected fresh fish. The first take should have warned me that things were not quite normal. It was a tug and a fast wiggly run which had all the marks of it being a foul-hooked fish. I returned the fish, not badly damaged at all, and I fished on. The next take was the same and again the foul-hooked hen went back in. This was, quite unbelievably, repeated several times and in the end I reeled up and left the fish – that colony of viragos – and sought saner fish elsewhere. It is always embarrassing to foul-hook a fish, or nearly always. I did once foul-hook a fish on floating line in Loch Maree, and that was curious rather than embarrassing, but to fish a pool and touch a fish with the fly I find very off-putting. I have had a small number of inexplicable foul-hookings in my time including a fine springer on the Brora which I returned almost with an apology to the salmon. But to hook fish after fish or – should I not put it the other way? – to have fish hook themselves in some kind of kamikaze event was a moment of madness which has stuck in my memory and still embarrasses me.

Fish can go peculiar in hot weather, for example during thunderstorms. I describe elsewhere in this book the difficulties of taking grilse packed into pools in the middle Dee when the water temperature rose to 70° Fahrenheit. It is a wonder the heat did not kill them. The rises these fish made in the evening were tremendous – pools alive with head-and-tailing fish – and as I waded in and stood casting fish after fish toured up past my legs. The pool was in a state of madness, but it was the madness of near extinction. In much the same way, salmon which are affected by disease, say UDN, will rise and leap and skitter and wallop madly, but wholly explicably. They will also upset healthy fish in the pools with their behaviour. I do not know whether this is because the fresh fish fear the disease or whether the untypical action of the affected salmon makes the healthy fish feel insecure. I usually love to see salmon show in the pools, because you can tell something about the state of the fishing as a result, but I hate to see UDN skittering, or even the wagging of the tail of an affected fish. That is the first sign usually. Sometimes an early sign of disease is a crashing leap, where the fish enters the water on it side and skates as it goes back in. No, that form of madness is the frenzy associated with disease and it is nasty, depressing and, as far as fishing success goes, wholly negative.

Happier forms of madness include salmon coming again and again to a fly they have missed. I have certainly seen a salmon rising seven or eight times to a fly and missing it on all but the last try, then getting it firmly. It may be that this is explained by some quirk of the light and the salmon has in fact been rising to a reflection of the fly on the mirrored undersurface of the water. I know sea trout do this. Indeed, it may bc one of the reasons why sea trout miss the dap so often. I have seen summer salmon – one in the Nith comes to mind – rising time after time to a greased-line fly and just not taking the fly at all, yet clearly interested in it and attracted to it. I have seen the loch salmon of the Highlands which rise to your fly as if they were attached to a spring on the loch bottom, like a practical joke toy. That is not so much madness as whim, or fickleness or edginess and staleness mixed. Salmon fishing is full of this. Real madness is quite distinctive. It is unpredictable and usually productive behaviour where salmon throw off their inhibitions, drop their guard, and take our flies wildly. If it were to happen too often it would spoil salmon fishing. In small doses – which is really all you ever get – salmon madness is unforgettable.

19

Welcome But Infuriating Grilse

When grilse come in to Highland rivers, usually during late July and August, they are most welcome. They ginger up the summer fishing and provide daytime sport in pools in which earlier salmon have now become coloured residents. They provide the chance of brisk sport, for a change, with multiple offers, plucks, takes and landings. But they also cause much hair to be pulled out in frustration. Rising, hooking and holding them affects the language of some salmon fishers and drives others into moods.

Grilse, the newest generation of returning salmon, seem to be on one of their cyclic upsurges in the mid-eighties. This

130

happened in the sixties, when some phenomenal catches of grilse were made on such rivers as the Thurso, the North Esk and the Tweed, and there seems to be every chance of it happening again. It is interesting that some people complain when grilse numbers rise substantially. They argue that grilse form one possible crop in a salmon river and that an excess of fish returning as grilse produces too many small fish on the redds, and perhaps breeds further grilse, where we would like larger summer salmon. Why some fish return as grilse with only one short burst of sea feeding before returning we do not know. We would love a proportion of grilse to stay several months longer in the sea and produce small springers of seven pounds or so, or to stay one further year at sea and produce springers of the ten-to-fifteen-pound class. What induces fish to return is not fully understood. There is a suspicion, however, that large grilse runs follow heavy stocking programmes on some rivers. One of the examples quoted is the remarkable crop of grilse and summer fish produced on the North Esk after a scheme of heavy stocking and careful net management organised there in the mid-sixties. But rivers such as the Dee, which is currently enjoying huge runs of grilse, have not been singled out for special stocking. In summers with low water, some anglers argue, grilse form a bonanza catch for the estuary nets and only small numbers of fish actually make the return to the pools and streams of the river. There are some fears that grilse form a kind of netsman's fodder crop, shared only in summers of high water with the anglers upstream. I am sure it is true that summer nets on occasion take huge quantities of grilse, but I am equally sure that some of the recent runs I have seen in the Dee particularly represent a fascinating angling opportunity which offers sport in summer months, long after the springers have gone off and well before the autumn runs begin.

I went up to Aboyne in mid-July 1983 in a heatwave. Half the village seemed to be bathing in our top pool at Aboyne Bridge and, looking in the shimmering heat over the low Dee, I wondered if I might not be a little optimistic in expecting any kind of salmon fishing in the river. I had booked the beat the following week and I rolled up the Saturday before to see what had been happening. I met a friend leaving the beat at lunch time, packing up not because the fishing was poor but because he had to travel back home during the day. He had taken three fish that morning and had had ten fish to his rod during the week. In his bag there were several fresh grilse as well as summer salmon. He asked me to fish his rod that afternoon.

There are times one wants to run to the riverside and begin. Indeed, in my boyhood, there were times when I did just that. Sometimes I would put up my rod as I walked down to the river, lest I should waste time setting the tackle up once I got there. So I made good speed that day to the Lummels, that magnificent pool on the Aboyne and Birse waters, and I set up my eleven-foot rod, with a size 10 Stoat's Tail and Silver on eight-pound nylon and began at the head. I saw two fish in the white water, but I don't think my fly was fishing the fast stream properly. It didn't feel right until I was about halfway down. Then, almost predictably, there was a little bulge and the sensation of a break and I was into a grilse. It all seemed easy. The rod bent well into the fish, which began twisting and running up the side of the stream. Then, quite unexpectedly, the fly came unstuck. With a little boil and a silver flash, the fish was gone. I felt empty.

I pulled another fish a little further down, but didn't hook it. Small flies. Was my fly too small? Yet I knew that all the other fish that week had been taken on small flies like this, and I also knew that those who had tried larger flies had had nothing. No, the fly was probably all right. Perhaps I was not giving the fish time? But how could that be? I was letting the fish take line off the reel when they pulled – the best way to make sure the fly is not pulled away from them as they take. I moved down to the fast Red Brae Pool below, a magnificent pouring stream. It is usually far too fast to fish well, but in summer, when the river shrinks and shows its bones, the Red Brae Pool reveals that it is a whole series of small, fast streams which lie masked for most of the season by the weight of water which flows through the neck. I kept well back, let the stream pull my fly round and hang it in the fast water, and I watched for fish moving. I saw two, then had an offer. The stream parted and a small fish took the fly in a most deliberate way. The line tightened, and yards were drawn off the reel in a sharp sudden run as the fish took. I raised the rod and was into the fish only for seconds. The hooks had failed to hold. I did not know what to say, but John, the ghillie, may have said it all for me: 'That's grilse for you.'

I went on to move five fish that afternoon and failed to get the hooks home in any of them. I cannot disguise the fact that I was, as usual, completely thrown by this. What made it more galling was that fish had been taken in the morning, and during the afternoon the other rod, fishing the same water as I was but using a long rod, took a fine thirteen-pounder and later in the day took two others. He, interestingly enough, was not taking grilse. I have no doubt at all that my fish were clean, small fish. His were all over ten pounds. It really is extraordinary. I expected grilse to take, and they did, but left me fishless. Was I willing them to come, rather than other salmon? No, that's too weird a theory. Something was happening and I think it is to do with my using, that day, my small eleven-foot rod in streamy conditions. The other rods had fished their fourteen-footers and I wondered whether they were thus able to present the fish with a slower fly, by holding the long rod up and fishing it slowly through the stream.

My week came, and I found the weather even hotter and the Dee falling to amazingly low levels. Yet the pools were full of grilse. The thermometer was unbelievable. During the day, the Dee temperature rose to 70° Fahrenheit. More and more people swam in the Aboyne Bridge Pool, and I didn't blame them. Fishing was reduced to morning and late evening and the displays of head-and-tailing grilse in the river were memorable. The Red Rock Pool was absolutely full of grilse. As the light went, I tried my tiny fly over the glide at the head and, first time down, a fish rose neatly to the small fly as it came round, but I felt nothing. As I waded, I could see grilse touring the pool and passing me by as they moved up the warm shallows. Over in the deep stream, I kept rising fish, so I increased the size of my fly. The same thing happened, but I noticed that the bigger the fly, the more vigorous the rises became. The night was by now darkening and it was really sea-trout time, but the salmon were still tantalising me. I should perhaps have left the Red Rock and tried the Stone stream above, but I was fascinated. The glide looked wonderful, and the fly came round perfectly. Every so often a silver line would appear behind the fly as a fish moved to me, but not once in the whole tense hour that the light lasted did I have even the sensation of a touch. I did take one sea trout and I did, on a faster stream at dusk, pull a salmon, but we had only three salmon for the week, and three or four sea trout, in complete contrast to sixteen salmon and some sea trout for the previous week.

Let me tell you how one of my guests managed it. He had agreed to fish a day and an evening and since he was very keen and had come a long way I allowed him to fish as late as he wanted to and, if he fancied it, to fish the morning of the next day, since we were on the same water and were spoiling nobody's fishing but our own. He had the same frustrating experience as I had. Fish after fish rose or moved or ignored him, but not once did he feel anything. He was at the end of his tether and, to mark the umpteenth and definitely final run through the Lummels, he put on an outrageous 1½-inch bright yellow tube. He said he watched it coming round in the water and thought how totally incongruous it looked in the low river. Well, you've guessed it. Halfway down a nice six-pounder took it – no messing about, a fine solid take with the hooks well in. It is nice to see one's guests getting fish, but isn't it the limit? Grilse. Sometimes I think they were sent to try us.

I often pick up sincere grilse in cooler summer weather just before the sea-trout rise comes on in the dusk. On the Spey there is a definite chance of this down some of the long glides, and on some of the pool tails just before the sea trout make their first rises to the fly. Again, one sometimes loses a grilse in these circumstances, but very often not. I can usually tell when the first pull of the evening is a grilse. It is so businesslike. It lacks the touch of the sea trout, and, when the hooks go home, it certainly lacks the fire of the sea trout in the fight. Spey grilse are often quite small, from three and a half to five pounds in weight. Some of them are lean little fish, with thin flanks and finely forked tails. A sea trout of the same size would fight far better, but there is a great deal of satisfaction in laying out a mixed bag for the dusk, all taken on the same size 8 sea-trout flies or on one of the small Waddington lures I used in the dark.

On lochs, grilse are splendid summer takers, especially in the mad first few days when they have just come up from the sea. They go for wet flies, of course, but they also go very well for the dap. It is interesting to hear from one Hebridean authority that he takes more salmon on the dap, meaning more grilse and small summer fish, than he takes on the wet fly. It is all part of the vigorous grilse syndrome. Being small, they can take with fast movements. They are notorious pluckers at the fly and I am beginning to suspect that they are very rapid spitters out of the fly too. Like many salmon fishers, I preach that flies should be presented slowly, or at least steadily, and that the reaction to the take should be either nothing at all, except a raising of the rod to fight the fish, or a slow tightening after the fish has turned. It works well with most salmon, but grilse seem to act far more like brown trout. I am not sure whether the best fisher for grilse would not be a young chap with a single-handed rod, and reflexes like electric sparks. He will lost salmon generally, but I think he will wipe my eye, and that of many other experienced salmon fishers, when the grilse are in.

I have recently had some correspondence with anglers about hooking summer fish, and particularly hooking grilse, and two of my correspondents, quite independently, advocate a large light fly fished with movement. One pattern much favoured is the Collie Dog – that extraordinary tube fly tied on polythene about an inch and a half long, but leaving three or four inches of hair trailing in the stream. The hair of the dog is curly and in the hand these creations look ridiculous. Yet I know they work well north of Inverness. I have heard great tales of their prowess on the Oykel, the Brora, the Helmsdale, the Thurso and the Naver. The Collie Dog also works well in spring in that area, even if it is a very light fly for cold water.

The other similar fly recommended to me is a lure, with a single size 4 low-water hook with an extended shank. The dressing is of long blue and black hair and the body is silver tinsel. I have no doubt this would work well for sea trout, but fished in low water it is astonishing that it ranks as a good taker of grilse and summer salmon. The inventor of this lure fishes it deep in low water – something I find a contradiction. Yet he takes fish, which I clearly do not. I am actually reminded by that lure of one of the time-honoured lures recommended by Arthur Ransome and others – the Vulturine Guineafowl lure. I have one precious example of this fly. It is light and is tied with a hackle from the cape of the African vulturine guineafowl which forms not so much a wing as a streamer. It is tied on a small Waddington, and it looks good. But I have to say that although I used it in the tepid pools of Dee in the hot summer of 1983 all I got were larger rises to it than to other flies.

Grilse excite me. They are beautiful, sprightly fish. But I clearly have a lot to learn about them, because they are always getting the upper hand with me. Perhaps a summer or two with high water and lowish temperatures – just the sort of summer we used to have when I was a boy – will bring me half a dozen sincere four-pounders and I will feel a little less frustrated by the waves of grilse which are now populating our summer rivers.

20

The Quest for Wild Trout

A great many advantages have been derived from the growing popularity of trout fishing. New waters have been created, new facilities of every kind – access, boat-houses, boats and even wheelchair pavements – have appeared as a result of the boom. Lochs which were once neglected are now stocked and managed. Protection Orders are on the increase, allowing investment in trout fisheries to be protected. Trout fishing on both sides of the Scotland–England border has increased vastly in resources, in scope and in shared enjoyment. From being a sport for English gentlemen only, in that country (but for every Scot who cared to wield a fly rod), trout fishing has now become generally shared.

In this development, however, it has lost something of its

quality. I do not propose to argue pro and con whether the new popular trout fishing of the last few years has been, on balance, better or worse for the sport. One aspect of the change does intrigue me, however – the loss of wild trout. I suppose what I am saying has a parallel in the one-time loss of real ale to the beer fanciers of Britain. They have restored that, because it is a product controlled by a human process. Wild trout fishing, alas, exists because little or no human interference takes place to change what nature herself has done.

This is, of course, a grossly idealistic viewpoint and is tinged with nostalgia. In practice it is almost impossible for wild trout to exist in Britain untroubled by the hand of man. Industrial gases blow through the entire atmosphere; mildly or severely acid rain falls on the just and the unjust, or if you like on the stocked and the unstocked water. Very few moors remain undrained, or have not been planted in some way likely to affect the trout in the streams and lochs we would like to call wild. So what is a wild trout?

As I see it, there is a difference in sporting quality between fish stocked as fingerlings or larger and trout which have been spawned in the local streams and have established themselves as the indigenous stock of the water concerned. The spawning success of the latter is dictated by local conditions, their survival rate as fingerlings is controlled by local predations and local food supply, their average size is the product of the available food and the efficiency of the trout in assimilating it. Trout which are naturally bred and self-regulated seem to me to give a much higher quality of sport and to produce a much better table fish at the end of the day.

The contradiction in my case is obvious. I am describing a wilderness trout community which I propose to discover and fish! We the anglers, are the intrusive influence. So let me modify my case a bit. All I am saying is that we want to enjoy fishing for trout as a kind of crop of nature rather than a crop of nurture. We might as well redefine wild trout, then. What I and many others continually seek is trout fishing, usually in still water, where there is no put-and-take stocking policy, where management concentrates on helping nature to produce a fitter and more attractive stock of fish from an angling point of view, and where we might have sport of a special quality. What I am

138

asking for is not the wilderness trout, but the unstocked trout loch where fish which have grown from spawning in the local streams provide fly-fishing of quality.

What is this quality I keep hinting at? It is epitomised by the unstoppable half-pounder. Have you noticed how astonishingly active fish of this size, from eight to ten ounces, are when they are wild-bred as opposed to stocked? My definition of a good wild fishery would include an average fish of this size. There are still hundreds of Scottish lochs where they can be found. Let me name some. Loch Frisa on Mull is a marvellous example. In the course of a day there – a day I had with Ian Neale of Dervaig one June recently – we took twenty-five trout. The best two fish were around a pound, but the most frequent fish were about ten ounces. They were free-rising but wary, and they seized the flies with a vigour which seemed disproportionate to the weight of the fish. When the pounders took the fly, they felt massive and were treated in the fight and in the netting with twice the care we would allocate to a ten-pound salmon. In fact, they took more fishing to bring to the net than a small salmon, allowing for the tackle used. Loch Frisa is not stocked, although I cannot guarantee that it has never at any time been stocked. I suspect that it has not, and is in the kind of state of nature, or near nature, I defined above. Its drifts are down rocky Hebridean shores with rowans here and there and that mixture of bracken, grass and rushes you come to expect. One side is a planted forest. It is hard to find unplanted lochsides these days. Long, finely rippled drifts are possible on Frisa and trout come and go as more or less fertile water is covered.

Another natural loch with all the qualities of wildness is Loch Rimsdale in Sutherland. If you drive up the glen in which the Helmsdale river runs – the Strath of Kildonan – and continue along the road which will eventually lead you to Strath Naver, you will come to the group of lochs usually referred to as the Badanloch waters, because they lie on that estate. A whole series of lochs lie in the hills here, to the north-east and to the south-west of the road. Similar lochs lie north and east of this point too, up the Kinbrace road to Forsinard, and, in a rich profusion of other waters, trout lochs lie still further north into Caithness. This area is possibly the best wild trout fishing of Scotland. You can walk to small productive hill waters, or you can fish larger but still wild waters within a few yards of the road. It is wonderful remote landscape, gentler in its contours then the territory to the west where Sutherland takes on the character of a Scottish Interlaken. From the Badanloch on a clear day you can see what Housman calls 'the blue remembered hills', but instead of seeing them sadly in the mind's eye, as he did, you can contact them, walk them, and fish among them. In the lochs there you will find what I call real wild trout.

Loch Rimsdale lies to the south of the Badanloch loch itself and it is connected with that water at its far western end. There is thus a great U-shaped loch – Badanloch with Loch nan Clar at its western end and, through a narrow neck, Loch Rimsdale lying is the next valley. The U-shape embraces the smaller Loch Fearnan, itself an excellent trout water. Rimsdale has reaches and bays I have not yet seen, where there are large trout which in May and early June can be tempted to take a dap. I have heard of six- and seven-pounders taken in this way there. The part of Rimsdale I know best is the southern end, reached by the little road from the Badanloch which runs over to Loch Choire Lodge, passing Fearnan on the way. This end of Rimsdale is shallow, sandy and open. It is fed by the burn which comes down from Loch Truderscaig, and by other small waters and, as far as I can discover, this sandy open end of Rimsdale is one great trout drift. The fish are there in plenty and they range in size from half a pound to two pounds and over. I have never had one of the large fish there, but once while fishing it with my teenage son I saw him take a fine trout of about a pound and a half. It is the kind of water where you would expect to take a couple of dozen trout in a day, unless conditions were against you. Over the golden sands, these trout take on a marvellous colour. They are rich yellow on the belly, deep brown on the back, and have beautiful large spots. When I talk about wild trout, I mean trout like this. I also mean places like this – clean, uplifting and inspiring glens with moorland and hill rising away on each side.

Wild trout are usually left unmanaged, because they are virtually unmanageable. If you have a reservoir in the Lowlands where you have control of the stock, you can carefully work out how many to put in each year, and of what size. You can decide how many you want to take out by fishing each season, and what the limits will be for size. There is no spawning available, normally, so allowing for natural losses you can calculate what restocking programme to undertake. Now, I fish waters like this and get lots of fun from them. In the next chapter I write of the excellent trout fishing of Gladhouse, for example. I have enjoyed Coldingham and Fitty and other waters. I do not deride carefully managed and stocked waters like this. What I am singing the praises of is trout fishing where the size and the quality are products of the environment.

Sometimes the environment produces a fishery which is not worth while. Years ago when I was spending a summer holiday on the island of Eigg I fished three lochs near the famous Sgurr of Eigg. One was nicknamed 'the breakfast loch' because it produced an interminable series of quarter-pounders and could be relied on to produce fish virtually to order. 'How many trout do you want for breakfast?' 'Oh, seventeen, about this size.' 'Right. I'll be back in half an hour.' That loch was as much a product of its environment as the Kidney Loch nearby where the only fish I ever rose and hooked was in the order of three pounds. In between lie other lochs, among them one we nicknamed the boomerang loch (Caol na Corn-Bhienne), which produced fish between three-quarters of a pound and a pound. Another loch only two hundred yards away from that produced several large swirls on a fairly cursory first fishing and yielded one trout of a pound and three-quarters.

Lochs can revert to tiddlers if left to nature, or, for complex but still natural reasons, produce fish of several pounds weight. Peculiarities exist throughout the trout loch spectrum. Loch Glutt in Caithness, near Altnabreac, has no apparent spawning and it produces trout of several pounds weight at their best. Is there anything less than two pounds in it? But I have walked many a hill on the way to a trout loch and have fished the little dhulochans which you will find on the moor regularly – small reed-fringed waters, dark in colour, usually without any spawning burn associated, but just filled by water oozing from the peat – and I have sometimes found them empty, perhaps because of excessive acidity, or have found them full of little dark fingerlings, soft in flesh and skinny in profile. Remoteness does not mean good trout, nor does the presence or absence of spawning burns.

The quest for wild trout, then, is an opportunistic one. There are no fixed characteristics of water to look for. It is true that well-known waters like Frisa and Rimsdale exist and should be enjoyed, but there are many waters hardly touched by fishers, nearly all requiring a bit of hill walking and some careful map reading. When you find them, some will fulfil your dreams and produce fish of great quality and memorable sporting experiences. Others, equally remote and equally endowed, it would seem, will have their own overpopulation problem, or their own naturally produced acid pollution. Finding out is, as in other quests, half the fun.

21
Tuesdays on Gladhouse

My staple diet of stillwater trout fishing comes through fishing Gladhouse Reservoir, in the Moorfoot hills south-east of Edinburgh. For a number of years I have had the good fortune to organise a small syndicate there, fishing one of the boats still held by local estates. Tuesday each week is my day. Gladhouse is fished in a minor way only by the boats put on by the two estates and the water is fished by Lothian Regional Council as the main fishery owners. A number of boats can be hired for day and evening fishing through the Council and Gladhouse has become a popular and well fished ticket water as a result. It is well managed and thoughtfully run and, in my opinion, is one of the best stillwater fisheries in the east of Scotland.

Fishing a loch consistently over the years gives you a different perspective on it from that of the casual day angler. There is a broad rhythm in each season, rather like farming, and the season-to-season variations are fascinating. There is, however, a negative side to regular fishing. Of course you get to know the water very well. Certainly, you know the depths and the drifts and where the larger fish might be at a given time during the season. But you do become slightly blasé about the fishing. You fish it more selectively, perhaps at certain hours of the day only, or taking the boat out only for the evening rise. It is all too easy, when you know you are likely to be on again in a week's time, and the weather is a bit gusty or slightly cold, to restrict your time out. I am sure I have lost all kinds of productive drifts by assuming that the overhead conditions were not right and postponing my starting time. For instance, one day recently in bright sun I decided not to go up until evening and I asked a friend to have a go during the day. Under a blazing sun he came on a rise of trout doing what you would not expect fish to do in glittering sun. They were steadily on the rise at the surface, taking small black flies and coming well to his cast. Unpredictable and almost unbelievable, but it is a regular experience for me to find that my predictions for the fishing have been, yet again, wide of the mark.

Gladhouse is a beautifully set water, lying hard against the northern slopes of the Moorfoots. It lies about 800 feet above sea level, which is a slight disadvantage since it can produce evenings which can chill quickly. The Moorfoots are bare hills, grassy for the most part and heathery on top. Gladhouse, as a result, gets most of the wind that is going. There is not a great deal of shelter from its banks, although the Arniston boat-house bay has a stand of old pines to the south-west – the main direction of the wind – and plantations of new pines on that bank and on the promontory we call the Cape of Good Hope give some small measure of shelter. The loch has two islands, each with stands of fine old trees and good undercover. As on many Scottish lochs, it is the islands which give you a clue to what the whole landscape would look like, but for sheep. Gladhouse islands are often blessed by the anglers, because somewhere round their well treed shores you can find shelter from the stormy blast and in that shelter you often find concentrations of rising trout.

I remember one June evening when we managed to get the boat up from our end of the loch to the shallows round the island which lies furthest west. We had hardly arrived there when the wind stiffened and we were in danger of being blown back down the loch a deal faster than we had managed to pull up. We found the trout difficult to move on our ordinary-sized loch flies, yet we could see the fish showing in the wave. I had seen conditions like this before and to match them I tied on a size 8 Loch Ordie, a small dapping fly with bushy hackles looking like a brush. On the bob this skipped and skated madly in that wind and it was tremendous to see fish pursuing it as if there were no tomorrow. They were good fish too, around the pound mark, and I had four or five in quick succession. The bag for the evening was, I think, about nine, and the fish came wildly and well. Gladhouse winds, however, often rob you of sport, partly because they keep you off the main drifts, and partly because, up on the Moorfoots, you get wind scud. I am sure every loch fisher knows what I mean. A loch is rippled by the wind and, as the wind rises, or if the loch has a reasonable reach, waves form. All this is good news to Scottish loch fishers. Wave and ripple, up to a certain height, provide ideal drifting and fly-fishing conditions. The wind, however, can bring a third surface effect – scud. You can see it happening as you drift. Sudden blasts of wind darken the surface of the loch and mottle the pattern of wave and ripple. The scuds are usually produced by a rising wind, or a wind which refuses to settle to a steady blow from any quarter. Westerlies with rain in them can be horrible for scud and if the wind turns to the north-west it makes me want to go home from Gladhouse. Our north-westerlies usually come with a pretty nasty package attached. The sky clears to a pale blue which, in the evenings, carries a yellowish tinge. Clouds are often white columns with trailing grey bases moving quickly over the sky. Showers are sudden, cold and heavy and the wind blasts from different northern angles without warning. The combination of unsteady winds, chilling of the surface with scuddy blasts and falling air temperature can ruin trout fishing.

What I like on Gladhouse is a gentle grey evening, steady from the south-west. I do not mind a drizzle of rain or a soft shower or two. I like to see the water with that dark-grey look, with slicks on it – those rather strange 'roads' over the ripple where the water flattens as if held down by oil. Slicks and the wave immediately beside them are tremendous places for evening trout. The slicks hold the hatching nymphs in their surface film and trout cruise up and down sucking them in. The water to the sides of the slicks offers the hatching flies easier conditions and there the trout will often rise in a splashier way to surface flies or flies just about to emerge. The rises in the slicks, however, are often dimples, little boils, surreptitious noses poked through the surface. In these conditions on Gladhouse, the drift has to be set just right. You can be ten yards too far to the left or right and miss your chances. We keep adjusting the drift down slicks, either by manipulating the drift anchor or by using the oars. The place I aim for is not the slick itself, but the wave ten yards to the right of the slick. I think sailors would have an accurate name for this position. From it, both rods can cover the water on their side of the slick and the slick itself, and the rod nearest the slick can usually put a long line over to the rough water on the far side. Slicks are seldom more than six or eight feet wide.

We fish Gladhouse from the beginning of April, wind and weather permitting. Some of the best early fishing we have had has been with snow on the ground. Some of the worst early fishing we have had has been because of scuddy north-west winds – March running on into April and, dare I admit it, May. In the earliest season we look for sheltered corners, places where a little microclimate produces water less chilled on the surface, or less rippled than the loch itself. It is very often profitable to think in terms of microclimate on a loch. I dare say I stretch the term a little in using it in this way. Microclimate is the weather in special environments. For example, the temperature and humidity at the bottom of the stalks of wheat in a field is a microclimate of the greatest importance to the crop. It can blow hard overhead, but down there it can be cosy. Similarly on a trout loch, you can find shelter, perhaps a deep bay with trees hard down to the shore, which we have on the south side of our boat-house bay, where trout will come in from the main loch and rise well in deep but sheltered water. Normally I would give water over ten feet deep a miss in my drifting, if I could. Here, in water which goes down to many times that depth, in wind which kills the main loch, we find relatively calm conditions and a bunch of good trout cruising round and taking wet fly sometimes, and dry fly often.

On Gladhouse we have several reaches with good weeds. Now, you might ask, when are weeds good? In my experience, weeds are good nearly all the time on Gladhouse. They mark out the shallower water; they cause an interesting little microclimate, sheltering the drifts beside them; they support fly life and they are splendid places for summer-evening sedges. Weed near deeper water often attracts larger fish which come in for security as well as food. On Gladhouse, where we have had a history of fluctuating levels until recently, because it is part of Edinburgh's drinking-water supply, we had many places where promontories on the loch shore would become new islands. Bankside grasses would become new water weeds, and normally inaccessible burn mouths would be driftable with the tufts of vegetation normally on the burn banks becoming part of a new geography of the loch and providing special little corners of their own climate. Since the new reservoir at Megget was formed in 1983, Gladhouse has been kept at its high level and the result is a mini-boom in feed from worms and other zoo input from the flooded banks. I have found some of these new shallows excellent for late-evening fishing.

Like many other Scottish lochs, Gladhouse starts its year depending on the small dark midges in their various forms. The term 'midges' is not a very satisfactory term for anybody, let alone anglers. Even to say, as some of the angling writers have, 'non-biting midges' is not particularly acceptable. I would rather use the scientific name 'chironomids', even if it sounds a little up-market. In strictly angling terms, of course, lots of us merely refer to the fly we use – the Blae and Black or the Black Spider or the Black and Peacock spider. It may sound jocular to the entomologist, but it is completely comprehensible to the loch fisher to say that there was 'a good hatch of Blae and Blacks'.

The chironomids form a very important part of the trout's menu in Scottish lochs from early spring onwards. You will see fish rising hard to them in calm water in mid-March. I remember walking down to the side of the Loch o' the Lowes (above St Mary's Loch in Selkirkshire) the first Saturday of the

147

trout season, round about 18 March, and seeing the nearly still loch alive with rising trout. With the shepherd's help I got our boat down to the water and spent a couple of hours trying to catch these trout, which were feeding hard on the little black midges which were everywhere. It must have been the first good fly feed of the spring for the fish and they were on a rising spree. The Loch o' the Lowes is over 800 feet up, as Gladhouse is, and it occurred to me that similar techniques to the ones I was familiar with on Gladhouse might do the trick. I tried normal wet flies fished carefully on the calm loch and got no offers. I switched to little black buzzer nymphs, in particular one called the Footballer, and got nothing. In desperation I turned to a small black spider fished dry and I managed to hook two fish before the rise went off. Ironically, both fish got off the very small dry spider before I netted them and I returned fishless to the house. I had, however, witnessed one of the phenomena of early loch fishing, one which I know well on Gladhouse – the early supply of chironomids.

The larvae of chironomids are deep-water creatures, quite a rare thing for loch flies. When the hatch takes place flies have a long way to go to the surface and I am sure that many are taken deep as ascending pupae. They stick in the surface film of still spring lochs on the days when we get nice warm mid-March or April conditions – often after heavy snow, for example – and they form excellent surface food for the hungry spring trout. The chironomid should be called the angler's friend, because the fly hatches well even in quite cold conditions in spring, and it is often the only fly around at the time. There are two maximum hatching periods for the black midge in Scotland. The first is early spring, March and April, and at that time the best hatches are to be found in the middle of the day. In still conditions, as I have described, the hatched flies often linger for quite long periods on the surface and trout cruise around and suck them in. This is a great time for a well fished small dry fly. To some anglers the dry fly is only for balmy summer evenings, or for

148

days on the loch when the wind fails. I have more and more come to think of the dry fly as a most likely tactic for the earliest weeks on river or loch in Scotland and, later in the spring and the summer, to be used some days as a general method of fishing, say with two on the cast, when there is ripple as well as when there is calm.

When the black midges hatch in spring they do so best in the middle of the day, but their other maximum hatching period is middle and late summer and then they tend to be evening-hatching flies. Of course, by this late date there is plenty of competition on the loch. Other flies abound and not many anglers concentrate on imitating the midges. Yet, in the summer of 1983, one of the most successful anglers on Gladhouse found that his size 16 Blae and Black took more fish than any other pattern and he had us all trying for trout with these tiny flies. It worked most impressively, despite the presence on the surface of a multitude of larger flies, including sedges.

The Blae and Black is a very interesting pattern. As you may know, it is dressed with a blae wing, a black body and hackle, a silver rib and a red tail. Some forms of the dressing allow a pheasant tip tail, but the one I use most often has a red feather fibre for its tail. This may seem to be just a decoration in the 'fancy' tradition of flies, but it is not. The larva of the black midges which we fish is coloured sometimes dark-red and sometimes blood-red. There is also an olive-green version. When these larvae (known as bloodworms) become pupae and rise to the surface their shucks are red in colour and, stuck in the surface film, they do give the appearance of black flies with a red tail. The Blae and Black is not so far away from this in form and colour.

I used to be very keen on buzzers, which is the name given to a range of chironomids when they hatch in summer. There were many patterns on the market: green buzzers, black buzzers, lovely nymphal patterns like the Footballer (dressed with a very midge-like body of alternate turns of white and black horsehair). I killed fish on the Footballer in Scotland, but I was wrong, I believe, to think that buzzers form much of the Scottish trout's diet. They are forms of chironomid found mainly on alkaline waters in England and in Ireland. Some of the buzzer nymphs I fished on stillwaters in England, when I lived for a

149

couple of years in eastern Essex, were huge. I remember a great day with a size 8 footballer nymph. It looked like an undressed hook, but with the football-jersey look down its shank and a tiny turn or two of herl at its head. Big rainbows walloped at it in one reservoir there near Torrington, in Suffolk. In turns out that some of the pupae of the chironomid in fat alkaline waters like that are an inch and a half long. On Gladhouse, our problem is that many of the midge pupae are microscopic.

Later in the spring on Gladhouse we get our share of the angler's curse, the *caenis*, known by all sorts of local names, some of them unprintable. The so called white midge is a hopeless creature for angling. It is, firstly, very small. It would take a size 18 or even a size 20 hook to represent it. There is one way we sometimes manage to represent it, however. We use a badger spider. As you will remember, the fibres of a badger hackle are creamy white at the tips and black at the roots. Thus a spider dressed from this feather gives a translucent image to the whole fly and a small dark-hackled fly seems to lie within. They say that trout see the inner fly in certain conditions and the fly within the fly takes them. It's a nice idea and there are times when it seems to work. I particularly like badger spiders dressed parachute-style for this fishing, that is with the hackle wound horizontally round the fly on a spike or bristle on its back. Try it. When the angler's curse comes on the water, any method which offers a chance of success is to be tried.

In fact there are said to be two forms of the angler's curse, noted particularly by J. R. Harris in that helpful book *An Angler's Entomology* in the Collins New Naturalist series. I am not sure if it is still available, but most libraries should have a copy. Harris says that the morning hatch of the caenis has dark legs while the evening hatch does not. The story about the badger hackles may actually have started because the pattern fished well in the early morning. An interesting idea. On Gladhouse, I have seen caenis hatching so thickly that our hats, bags and coats were white with them in a short time. The overabundance of nature. Trout feed varaciously on these flies and very rapidly become preoccupied and will look at nothing else. My way of staying sane is to wait until the dusk really comes down and fish ordinary flies along the margins of the loch. I have found that when darkness falls, even after gorging themselves on caenis, trout turn to large flies

and they take them well. The trout in Gladhouse, as elsewhere, are opportunists. When the light goes and possibly
small flies are hard to see, the fish feed on, but change to larger
targets.

The Tuesdays of Gladhouse form, I dare say, a representative
cross-section of the sport of the whole year. One of the bounties
of summer which I wait for each season is the fishing of sedges. I
recall my very first visit to Gladhouse as a young angler. We
fished an evening, and by luck I found a group of fish taking
sedges. In those days I did not have patterns of sedge flies in my
box, but I had a Greenwell with longish trailing wings and I had
a Dunkeld with tent-shaped, rather large wings. These did well
and I had four or five fish over the pound that evening, all
coming to the flies fished off the bankside reeds and moved
quickly by handlining. This works well on Gladhouse. I often
think that any dark fly with tent-shaped wings will be taken for a
sedge. After all, sedge fishing is done in the dusk, when profile
and fly behaviour is far more important than colour. Sedges are
bulky creatures in the forms we meet most in summer-evening
sedge fishing. I should add at once that I discovered with
surprise recently that there are sedges of all sizes and that many
of them are only about a tenth of an inch in length. Clearly the
sedges we use in our normal fishing are up to half an inch long
and I have longer versions in my box. Just how large sedges can
be was borne in on me one July evening on Ardleigh Reservoir
in Essex. I was bank-fishing and sedges were on the go.
Suddenly something the size of a Chinese dragon got into my
hair, just behind my ear. I panicked a little and tore off my cap
but found I could not get the dratted thing off my hair. When
eventually I did I found that it was a sedge, I think a great red
sedge, and it was about an inch and a half long and buzzed like a
band-saw. I believe these flies are called murraghs in Ireland.
Well, a pestilence on them too for panicking me!

The Gladhouse sedges are mostly cinnamon sedges or
silverhorns. I am sure you will have seen them on the loch, or
rather on the reeds and stones beside the water. They are
usually grayish or dark brown with mottled wings and they are
easily imitated using a grouse wing or even a woodcock, except
that the wing must be long enough to give the fly a ridge of
wings down its back. The body is usually generously dressed

from dark-brown dubbing and usually the hackles are wound down the body in palmer style. I have also fished dressings in which the hackle was added after the wings and tied like a ruff in front of them. On Gladhouse we fish the fly sometimes as a nymph, but most usually as a capering or motor-boating adult fly moving over the loch surface. I like anchoring the boat or having it held off the reeds where the sedge flies are hatching. It is not necessary to drift, and, indeed, it is usually counterproductive. The fish move up and down the margins of productive reed beds and the way to take them is to cast right to the reeds and strip the fly back off the reeds causing a little surface disturbance. The natural sedges cause a great deal of surface disturbance, and many of them leave a wake like a small power boat. I have noticed, however, on Gladhouse at least, that the trout begin the rise by being wary of the motor-boating sedges and preferring the nymph or the gentler surface flies. Later, you will see trout chasing and taking the surface caperers, even the great wake-making stormers. Trout are a little conservative at the beginning of a rise, I find.

Memorable things on Gladhouse include fishing the very last cast just off our boat-house on the way in after the dusk rise stops. One of my close friends, an excellent and innovative trout fisher, Bert Morris, has a remarkable technique for these last-gasp trout in the dark. He has had a series of very large single hook worm flies tied up. You will hardly believe that he fishes low-water 6s, tied fore and aft with furnace hackles and peacock herl. Worm flies are most usually fished as tandems, and are associated in my mind with heavily waved Highland lochs where the next take might be a salmon or a sea trout. On Gladhouse, the trout go very positively for Bert's large single worm flies, and when I say positively I mean that he can take half a dozen in quick succession, including some solid fish over a pound. Now if we had great red sedges there I would have no hesitation in saying that his fly worked like one. But we have none. Does it make the Gladhouse trout think they have landed already in paradise where flies are larger and more satisfying? I do not know. My larger flies do not do as well. The reason I have not fished these large flies at dusk very much is that I cannot easily convince myself that they are not too big. They seem incongruous on a trout rod. They would even be big for night sea trout. Yet the Gladhouse trout like them and, I think, take them for motor-boating sedges.

My Tuesdays on Gladhouse are marvellous. They take me to a peaceful hill water within twenty minutes or so of my home in central Edinburgh. The water has an average trout weight of about three-quarters of a pound, and it has given our little syndicate, each year for the past six, several trout well in excess of two pounds. Our best fish in that time was one of three pounds two ounces. Gladhouse trout are good to look at, being high-backed and well spotted and sometimes very yellow. They are strong fighters and are rather cunning. No sooner do I get the feeling that I know them than they change their behaviour and remind me that I am not much more than a visitor to their world, albeit a regular one. Some nights when I have had – and this is not a word of a lie – seventy or eighty rises with no fish hooked, I feel that I should start at the beginning again and ask myself: 'How do we really catch Gladhouse trout?' If I were to ask that question, even softly, one evening when I am alone in the boat, I am sure someone would glide up and give me his theory on how it all works. It would be like the survival instructions given to the Canadian Mounted Police, who were told that if ever they were lost in the wilderness they could summon help quite simply by saying aloud 'Now this is how you mix a dry martini . . .' and a voice would say at once, 'No it isn't; I'll tell you the right way'. Gladhouse, which I sometimes think I know well, keeps reminding me that whatever I know about fishing, it is only a tiny proportion of what there is to know. Gladhouse is thus a kind of archetype; it keeps its secrets well.

22

Going Barbless

If there is anything fundamental to fishing it is hooks. My left thumb will tell you that. It is my test-pad for hook point sharpness and the pattern of my thumbprint is broken in numberless places where I have tried a hook for needle-sharpness before tying it on to my cast. On the negative side, there are few disappointments so deep as finding that you have knocked the point off a favourite fly on a rock behind you as you cast. It happens, even to the most experienced, and the *frisson* of discovering that a good fly has become scrap because of a slack cast is sometimes misery itself. So far I have described the hook as if its point were all. A hook has two points, however: its point proper and its barb, the reverse point which holds it in once it penetrates. I look at barbs and I make sure they are proud of the hook, but I don't test them for sharpness. Hook and barb are, in my concepts at least, virtual inseparables.

154

A couple of seasons ago I had the opportunity to fish a rainbow pond at the Selcoth fisheries in the Moffat valley which lies just over the watershed on that lovely road which runs from Selkirk to Moffat, passing St Mary's Loch and the Loch o' the Lowes on the left as you progress westwards, then crossing the saddle of the hills near the Grey Mare's Tail waterfall and following the Moffat Water down. Selcoth have made a little loch there which they have stocked with rainbows, all of substantial size, running from about a pound and a half to three or four pounds. It is a very pleasant pond to fish on a nice evening with good fish nymphing – very different sport from the trout fishing I have had on the neighbouring lochs, St Mary's, Lowes and Skene.

One of the rules of the fishery is that you may take only two fish, but you are allowed to fish and return rainbows. Barbless hooks must be used, to prevent damage to returned fish. I have never fished barbless hooks except on Selcoth and when I first had to remove the barbs from a couple of my favourite nymphs I must say I felt with a pang that I was ruining excellent flies. The method suggested to me was to take a pair of fine-nosed pliers and press the barb down flush with the hook wire. It works very well. I do not think it would be possible to prise up the barb again. Hooks made barbless stay barbless.

Fishing without barbs worries you before you begin, but, when the fish are actually being cast to and hooked and played, you forget the barbs are off. I expected to have lots of missed rises, but I didn't. I missed a few, but no more than I would expect to with ordinary hooks. I found hooking just as easy or difficult as normal and there was no sense of anxiety at all. What was more surprising was that I found that fish did not fall off during the fight except in the normal proportions. Of course, when you are playing fish on barbless hooks you absolutely must keep in touch with the fish all the time during the fight. The same is true if you are using barbed hooks, but the barb gives you a small margin for error. Barbless hooks keep you on your toes.

Even leaping fish can be held well on barbless hooks, as I discovered much to my relief. Many of the Selcoth rainbows leapt vigorously during the fight, but stuck on well. I think what would do for you in fighting lively fish with barbless hooks

155

would be cart-wheeling. One rainbow I saw leaping there was lunge-leaping, that is leaping forwards against the pressure of the line and the rod. Even if rod pressure were released temporarily during the leap, there would still be good pressure on the hook from the line itself. I do not believe that dropping the point is always the right drill for dealing with leaping fish. When a fish chooses to leap, any reaction on the part of the angler is probably too late. This is especially true of big sea trout and of salmon. It is always the best fish which cart-wheel, too. I have had heart-stopping moments when fish over twenty pounds on one occasion and in the upper teens on others leapt and cart-wheeled alarmingly during the fight. Barbless hooks would not hold in these circumstances. Nevertheless, it was fascinating to find how effective barbless hooks were the first time I tried them with rainbows of two and two and a half pounds.

Some of my colleagues think that barbless fishing is unnecessary. A fish properly handled can be released with little or no scarring if ordinary hooks are taken out carefully. There is a lot in what they say. If the hand that grasps them is wet and if the grip is steady and firm the fish will suffer neither skin 'burns' not structural damage. If I am going to return a fish to the water, say a hen salmon in September, I try not to net the fish at all. If I can, I do not take the fish out of the water. I think nets take off scales sometimes and if fish get deeply bagged in nets, or if the hook fouls the net meshes, there can be delays and hard handling. What I do with salmon is to bring the fish into the side, preferably to a shingly or muddy beach, and push the fish by its tail until it is just out of the water. Then quickly I run my hand down the leader to the fly and push it down and back to release its hold. If the fish has engulfed the fly, it raises difficulties and fine-nosed pliers or forceps are required. I carry these in spring to release kelts. But it is surprising how many fish can be quickly and easily released in this way. Having released the fish, it should not be thrown back in. It should be placed in the water and held, if necessary, until it gets its balance and swims off. Salmon should be held and then pushed off upstream.

In the little loch at Selcoth, release was smooth and easy. Some of the fish were released without their bodies being touched at all. The rainbow was fought to a standstill at the edge.

Then the hand was run down the leader and the fly pushed out, and the fish was allowed to turn away untouched but safely unhooked. There is hardly any contact with the trout and, in the best unhooking, there is none at all. I am perfectly happy with barblessness on Selcoth pond, and, if I were pressed, I would agree to it on any water where there was a strict limit on catches, provided it allowed me to go on fishing after I had taken my limit. I would hate to go barbless for sea trout, or for wild browns. These fish fight in such a way that loss would almost certainly be high. As for salmon fishing, the fish itself is such a trophy, and is so expensive to fish for, that it would be daft to increase its chances of escape. Small fish on fly would probably come in quite easily on barbless hooks, but the best half-dozen fish I have taken in the last few years would certainly not. Barblessness should enhance our fishing, add zest, a sense of uncertainty, should sharpen our skills and should protect our returnable stock. When it comes into fishing as a crashing negative, and increases our frustration through losses of major fish, it is an unnecessary sophistication and should not be adopted.

23

Rainbow Beginnings

Scotland has come late into the rainbow stakes. In some ways, it has also marked its attitude to rainbow trout by getting out of developing them extensively. There are some very well known rainbow trout fisheries in the south of Scotland. Perhaps Coldingham Westloch, near St Abbs just north of Berwick, is the first water to come to mind as a successful rainbow fishery. It is a very interesting water, probably unique. For generations Coldingham has had the name of being a small loch which grows large trout and before rainbows were introduced some very large browns were taken there. There are still huge brown trout in the loch and from time to time lucky anglers take fish which rival the best brown trout from the fattest English stillwaters. Beside these substantial browns, Coldingham has some fine rainbows to offer. I used to love fishing for its two-pounders in March and early spring – virgin fish which seemed to have fed well right through the winter. These fish were great sport and, I have no doubt, still are. From time to time, fishing Coldingham in the summer, you would see miraculous rainbows from three to six pounds in weight, beautifully proportioned fish and sporting to the nth degree. If Coldingham was not in fact the first loch of all to stock the rainbow trout, it was one of the earliest and it has emerged as one of the great success stories of rainbow fishing in Scotland.

I must also mention two other waters where rainbows have been stocked and fished successfully in fisheries which can be enjoyed by wide numbers of anglers – Loch Fitty, near Dunfermline, and the Lake of Menteith, not far from Callander and Aberfoyle. Loch Fitty was rescued from being a neglected, pike-infested water by a small team of enlightened anglers, one of whom is Ian McKenzie. They have produced in Loch Fitty over the last twenty years a highly interesting and very sporting fishery based on rainbows, but with some excellent brown trout also in its waters. As a kind of fun extra, some American brook trout (*Salvelinus fontinalis*) have been introduced to the water and have provided interesting variety in the bags. Fitty is a lowland water, set in rich agricultural land, and, as you would predict, is rich in food. It is close to Loch Leven and it lies, to some extent, on the same rich bed – glacial clay, which has been enriched by lime. Fitty rainbows can grow large – six, seven or more pounds in weight – but the fishery is managed on a policy of producing a spectrum of weights, allowing fun with good numbers of pounders, reasonable chances of fish twice that weight, and occasional big fish to test your skill.

The Lake of Menteith was, again, a neglected water which was resurrected in the sixties and turned into a well managed fishery based on the stocked rainbow. Menteith had its pike and coarse fish too, and they have to be kept down. There were indigenous brown trout there, many of considerable size. Browns introduced to the water grow quickly and provide, as on Fitty, an interesting addition to the bag. Menteith has been selected for some of Scotland's major trout fishing competitions, in some ways replacing Loch Leven, which has had some serious problems with its brown trout in recent years. Although Menteith has, recently, started to re-emphasise the brown trout

159

in its waters, which suggests a slight disenchantment with the rainbows, it is still a major rainbow fishery which has worked well for some twenty years.

One could list others where the rainbow has thrived. For example, Portmore Loch, lying above Gladhouse in the western Moorfoot Hills not far from Edinburgh, has not only a name for giving good sport with rainbows of the two-pound class, but has produced some spectacular rainbows of six, seven and eight pounds in weight and is held to hold many heavier than this. I have seen some enormous rainbows in its waters while I have been fishing there. One barrel of a fish was brought in one night by a bank fisher. He had not caught it; it had wallowed in distress beside him. The fish appeared to be blind and was going back. He killed it and brought it in for examination. It weighed seven pounds and was as fat as a carp. To my salmon fisher's eye it was rather unpleasantly portly. Shouldn't real fish look like torpedoes?

There are many other waters where the rainbow has done well and many of them are quite small, stocked ponds. The Inverawe fisheries, for example, in the Western Highlands on the road between Dalmally and Oban, close to the River Awe, produce some corkers of fish into double figures. The Lily Pond there is a fascinating water and possibly it represents at once the most effective type of rainbow fishery, if you want big fish, and the most English of Scottish fisheries. Fish are stocked from the local rainbow fisheries, and some of the best fish there are grown to maturity in the salt waters of Loch Etive. It is interesting that rainbows are tolerant to a degree of salt in the water they live in and at least one English fishery I know, the Loom Pit, near Ipswich, runs on a policy of introducing brackish water from the nearby estuary to enrich the environment. In Loch Etive, the salt water is diluted by the fresh water of the Awe and other streams. It is a long arm of the sea and it possibly never becomes as fully salt as the Atlantic. At any rate, rainbows can be grown in these conditions to substantial sizes and they can be introduced to the Inverawe ponds for trophy hunters. I must not sound snooty here. I rather like Inverawe, and I do like some of the fishing I have had there, even if it is straightforward put-and-take fishing.

There is a problem generally with rainbows in Scotland,

however. They can do well, as I have argued, in certain types of water and they can provide good wild-type fishing as in Fitty, Menteith and Portmore, where you are hunting a fish which had become acclimatised to the water, has adapted to wild feeding and which continues to grow and keep good condition. Of course these are put-and-take fisheries, because rainbows do not breed there. But they are waters where the fish go on developing and growing. In ponds and the smaller lochs, where large fish are introduced, it is unlikely that the fish will maintain condition and develop, for the simple reason that the amount of food required to keep up large rainbows is prodigious. They are fantastic protein converters. If the food is there in any quantity, the fish will consume it heartily and will show good condition and growth. If, as is the case in many places, the water does not have the natural food which the rainbows need in abundance, the fish will rapidly lose condition and die off, unless they are fed artificially.

I have fished lochs in the Highlands where experiments have been tried by stocking extensively with small rainbows. In these waters, which have in the past been able to support a good stock of brown trout, with big fish among them, rainbows seem not to be able to find enough food. In quite a short time they begin to lose weight and turn dark in colour. They seldom survive the winter. One local fisheries scientist has called these the shrinking rainbows of the Highlands. Elsewhere, anglers talk about the disappearing rainbow. There is, of course, nothing wrong with fishery experiments. With the tourist development of the Highlands, improvement of loch fishing is seen as a very obvious project. Unfortunately, local clubs and consortiums of hotels were badly advised if they assumed that all that was necessary was to introduce vigorous fish-farm rainbows and wait for the fish to establish themselves and grow. Highland waters are, generally speaking, just not fertile enough to support rainbows. Further, rainbows may compete so well for the available food that the indigenous brown trout fare badly and go into decline.

In one way, I am sorry that Scotland should have turned out to be, on the whole, unsuitable for rainbow trout, because they are incredible creatures. I really got to know them when I was resident in Essex for a couple of years. They were interesting to catch, were often tremendous fighters, and really bent the rod well. They forced you to think differently in fly-fishing, too. For example, rainbows often move in small packs through the still or nearly still surface, making little wakes and bulges and absolutely vacuuming in the nymphs they find. There is sometimes an evocative little noise, like whispering, associated with these surface forays. Whispering rainbows! Brown trout cruise around just under the surface of the summer loch, but they do so largely as individuals, and they rise or bulge to the nymphs they take. Rainbows sometimes remind me of plankton feeders in the way they suck their way through the water, as if taking everything in and filtering it. Indeed, they may *be* plankton feeders, or feeders on the micro creatures associated with plankton. Whispering rainbows – may I use the term? – are not very easy to take, I find. To do well you have to predict where the pack will go next and try to get your nymph in front of them. On a large irrigation reservoir at Torrington in Suffolk we used to have tethered rafts to fish from. You pulled yourself out ten or fifteen yards from the bank on a kind of running moor line. It was marvellous to kneel out there and wait for the packs of fish to come past. They could be plainly seen on the quiet surface. One thing I learned right at the beginning was that these cruising packs were given to a logic of their own. They would appear and disappear quite suddenly. Packs would weave and turn on their tracks in what could be an infuriating way, because you could not easily predict where the fish would go next. Brown trout were far easier to deal with, I thought. To do well with rainbows in this mood, you had to be maximally flexible and quick in your presentation. I found it useful if I suddenly saw a movement of a fish to pop my fly right on its assumed nose and, if the fly was not taken in seconds, to change direction rapidly and look for another fish. It was sometimes quite frantic, or must have appeared so to an observer on the bank. Yet, with fitful feeding patterns, this kind of flexibility is necessary.

Rainbows are, in my view, great fish when they are taken on a floating line with a small nymph. What takes, what pulls you get! There is a high visual content in the fishing, and it cultivates a sharp eye and dextrous tackle handling. Fishing for rainbows with sunk lures can be rather tedious. Of course the largest fish are often taken right down on the bottom of the pond, but I think there is a great loss of sensitivity in the fishing. I do it myself, when conditions dictate, but give me half a chance to take fish on the surface, even fish which are substantially smaller than the bottom feeders, and I will take it like a flash. I remember being on Grafham one summer evening and there was not much moving near the bank. I was on the floating line with nymphs and some chaps not far from me were exploring the bottom with a well sunk lure. One of them got into a fish and I thought he was having rather a long fight of it, so I trotted along to see what was happening. He was fast into a great bream, which he eventually landed and weighed in at 9 lb 8 oz. He returned it, I think. What a great wet sack of a fish it was. He told me he had taken others almost as large. His bottom-seeking lure seemed to be quite effective for large, fat bream. I was interested, indeed slightly amused by this catch, but I do not think I want to emulate it.

It is significant that in England and in Scotland the best rainbow waters seem to be also the waters most troubled by coarse fish. This is almost certainly connected with water chemistry. With the exception of pike, which seem at times to thrive in fairly acid lochs in the Highlands, other coarse fish are found only in waters with neutral or slightly alkaline chemistry. This is one way of saying that rich waters support multiple colonies of fish, because the food is there. Trout, I mean brown trout, are well adapted to living in waters which are unattractive to coarse fish, where food is hard to find and has to be hunted relentlessly for survival. I shun slightly the rich, green waters of the lowlands where rainbows and perch and other coarse fish thrive. I am attracted to the trout in its wild and rather harsh waters, fighting for its life in a sparse environment. It is, somehow, like what happens on the banks of trout lochs. Heathery moors are not fat places. Life for all but the most vigorous and best adapted fauna is impossible. Agriculturally, not much can be done with an acid moor. You might graze a sheep per acre, or you might find that even that density was too much for the moor. Yet the deer thrive and, in the lochs, wild trout do well. I think it is my own national philosophy which is speaking here, wedded, as usual, with a rather idealistic form of romanticism. I will not go as far as to say that rainbows are bad

163

and brown trout good. The truth lies nearer the middle than that. Rainbows do not readily fit into the rather stark environment of Scottish trout lochs. When they are introduced, they seem to me to be out of place. Wild brown trout in Scottish lochs just seem to be much more worthwhile to catch, even if they are smaller, take more effort to pursue, and, in a sense different from rainbows, have to be hunted. When you meet me fishing Fitty or Portmore or one of the ponds at Inverawe, I will not be being hypocritical, however. I will be enjoying a rather exotic sport. The word is interesting. It means 'foreign'. Doesn't the word fit rainbows well?

24

The Essence of Tweed in Autumn

The Tweed is a popular and interesting spring river. It has its cycles and can produce, in some years, close to a hundred springers per beat for the month of February from St Boswells down. Not many rivers can match that. In terms of numbers of fish, that is coming close to beats on the Dee in a good April or a modest May. Yet the Tweed is not widely regarded as a crack spring river. It does not have the size of fish produced by the Tay, nor the quality of fish from the rivers of Inverness-shire and Sutherland. It does not have the Highland feel to its spring fishing, despite its productivity. It is, in a word, a lowland river and its spring fishing does not match the image of the sport – snow-capped hills, wintry glens and desolate moors – which goes with what we are pleased to call spring salmon, even if in tonnage of early fish Tweed is far ahead of some of the waters of the north.

At the other end of the season, however, in autumn, when Highland rivers are either full of stale fish or are closed for the year, the Tweed comes into its own and produces a quality of fishing which is so far above other waters for duration, size of fish and quality of sport that one could almost feel that we were faced with a different salmon from anything else known in Europe, offering sport in a unique environment. Heady words. Yet anyone who has had the privilege of fishing the Tweed in ply from September onwards might have felt this. It is like nothing else, anywhere. The river sweeps through its rich haughs and pours over its slaps and through its dubs and brings in more fish per unit of area than I have seen anywhere in Scotland. You could well think, at the least, that the Tweed was indeed part of the old Rhine and that its twenty- and thirty-pounders in autumn were a race apart.

Autumn begins on the Tweed, as far as most anglers are concerned, when the estuary and coastal nets come off in mid-September. That event sometimes feels like the opening of the gates of the river. If you have water then, the first run of the autumn, sometimes a fabulously productive run, can be in the pools of Tweed certainly up to the junction with Ettrick and even ten miles further than this by the end of the month. The coming off of the nets marks the beginning of the fly-only weeks of the autumn and, for me, the beginning of proper Tweed fishing. I do not want to suggest that the first-class summer fishings with floating line are not marvellous, nor do I entirely want to turn my nose up at the bait-fishing the Tweed can provide. I happen not to like spinning all that much, and on great slow pools of the lower Tweed bait-fishing can be somewhat tedious at times. What I mean by proper fishing is the sport the Tweed gives with its own race of flies, with sunk lines and long rods and, above all, big energetic fish. There is, frankly, no autumn fishing like it.

Sometimes, the autumn fishings on the Tweed start with a little hangover from the summer. Waters in September can be warm and low and fish may first of all be found in the streamier lies and may be taken on floating line with small tubes or with

166

size 6 doubles – flies which you might expect to take fish on from the end of April and right through the summer weeks, if there is water. Sometimes anglers are a little too keen to usher in the autumn and they take to the sinking line too soon. I know how they feel. They are eager to feel the big fly coming round through the stream and being stopped by a fifteen- or twenty-pounder. Once the autumn fish arrive, they will take your fly in this way. They will be in the streams and glides and, even if the water is moderately low, will take the bigger fly well. But if your autumn starts with a summery September of a warm, low early October, treat it like summer. In the first place, it is unlikely that the real autumn fish will be there, and, in the second place, salmon will almost certainly want to rise to the flies rather than have you take them down to them. I have seen this again and again in September and early October. Once, when rods were sinking the fly deeply all around him, a friend of mine took two magnificent October fish on a half-inch Stoat's Tail – a Dee fly! – and a floating line. Again, after a day on the Junction Pool at Kelso, with fish beginning to show up right at the end of September, I remember the ghillie at Bemersyde taking four fish in the evening from his own Boat Pool on a small virtually hairless tube fly tied on to polythene. Interestingly, the water was quite coloured that night. We were taking fish at Kelso on autumn flies, but the Bemersyde ghillie did better than any of us after tea with a wisp of a fly.

These conditions are not really autumn, however; they are the tail of summer. Usually autumn starts with the equinox in September. Around the twenty-first of the month we expect wind and, with luck, the first cool floods of the back end. They are often dirty floods, with lots of colour and with debris and soil suspended. The Ettrick does its worst and brings down cocoa-coloured water; the Leader goes sandstone-red, a fine colour if it is on a mansion house, like Dryburgh, but not welcome when it ruins the fishings on the Tweed. It is not unusual for there to be two quick floods to start a good early autumn on the Tweed. The first flood is small and dirty and it does little more than clean out the river and get rid of road washings and other muck. It also signals to the fish at sea that the time has come to run. If we get a rise in the water within a few days of this, excellent runs come in. They can go amazingly far in a day or so. One of the best runs I have ever seen in the Tweed came in during the last week of September 1982 and filled the pools of the river up to Galashiels. I was fishing Boleside, near Galashiels, just below the junction with the Ettrick and I had two fabulous days of sport before the Ettrick rose again and washed us out. I write separately about that event in the next chapter, because it was a remarkable event, a productive window in between two floods. It was a lucky event too, for me. I am very conscious of that. Any rod could have killed fish effectively in the perfect conditions I met on 30 September that year. It can be very different indeed around that time, however, as my fishing on Boleside showed the following year. The water was dead-low and stale. It had had little or nothing from the equinox. The rain which had come in September seemed to shun the south-east of Scotland. It flooded the Tay and the Highland rivers, many of which were on their last few days of salmon fishing, but it left the Tweed virtually at summer level. I did catch an autumn salmon in these conditions, much to my surprise. It was small and very fresh and it took a Waddington of about an inch and a half in length, fished on a slow-sinking line. I had had nothing on smaller flies in the conditions, although they looked like the tail end of summer, so I 'thought autumn' and fished the Hart Pool as if it were October. The fish took well, but my excuse for it is that it was fresh and might well have taken anything. The Tweed can be generous one year and stiff and dour the next, but the key to it all is water after mid-September.

During October the river cools rapidly and, while ice is not usual in October, it can certainly occur. There can be persistent cold rain in some Octobers, and there can be a lot of wind, which has a chilling effect on the water. This is often the best month of the whole year on the Tweed. The fish can come in strength, great silver fish from ten pounds to thirty pounds in weight. The October fish are fast runners, and excellent takers. They go right to the head of the river, filling pools as they go and bringing great sport to the upper middle river from Galashiels through Walkerburn and Innerleithen to Peebles. This run also brings fish to the Ettrick and its interesting tributary the Yarrow. In some autumns the bulk of the fish come in October. I have noticed that when this happens, as it did in 1983, for example, it is followed by a low November. Interestingly, when the Tweed runs persistently high for weeks on end through October and November, fish seem not to run in such great numbers, as if they know that they have plenty of time to get up. If you want to read of a remarkable case of this, I have tried to catch the flavour of the fishing in the falling water at the very end of November 1982 in Chapter 28. In contrast, in 1983 when fish ran in great numbers in the third week of October, and low water spoiled the fishings of November, leaving the river low and stale at the end of the month, the end-of-year run did not come until the third week of December, long after the rod season was over, and observers told me that fresh fish were still coming in over the cauld at Kelso on Christmas day.

November can bring winter. I have had some icy and difficult fishing on the middle and lower Tweed in this month, for example in the time I was in the little syndicate at Maxton, near St Boswells. In icy cold weather, a flood on the Tweed can take on a grey colour. I imagine this is caused by the land being frozen and staining the flood less with soil. I much prefer a brown flood, followed by tawny-coloured water, clearing to light sherry, if not gin, by the fourth or fifth day.

When salmon run the Tweed in bulk, as they often do, it is difficult to make the most of them. You have high days followed by sudden slumps. I love the smaller pockets of fish which I used to meet from time to time at Maxton in November. On the Embankment there I remember stopping for lunch with one rather dark salmon to show for my morning, when I suddenly saw a fish making a little sharp head-and-tail rise in the main pool. I was cold and bit tired and I said to myself that I would not get up and fish just because a salmon had shown, but if it were to show again in the same lie. . . . It did and I laid down the hot soup, stepped in, hooked a fish in the lie and landed it, a fresh eight-pounder straight from the sea. I fished the lie again immediately and had another absolute carbon copy of the take and the small shining fish. I went in again and this time it all happened as I hoped, but I broke in the fish. I blued the air. I had been fishing a tube I had tied up myself. What I think had happened was that the lining had sheared between the copper tube and my leader, perhaps during the fight when pressure on the nylon may have cut into the polythene liner. It is something I have spotted several times since and it is one good reason for

169

always fishing Waddingtons. I switched to a Waddington of about the same size and colour – yellow of course – and took a third fish, then it stopped. I went back to my soup and it was cold. Never was a lunch better sacrificed. I finished with a fifth fish and lost my sixth in the Minister's Pool that day. What a river the Tweed is in autumn.

There are no particular secrets about fishing the autumn waters on the Tweed, but you must come to something of an understanding with your tackle. Typically it is a fourteen-foot or fifteen-foot rod, glass or carbon, with a No. 10 sinking line and a Waddington or more likely a tube fly of up to two inches in length. I have said elsewhere that I am a slow-sink-line fisher. I do not like thin, fast-sinking lines which cut down through the water and which, if you handline much, cut your forefinger too. I despise lead-core lines. They are too often a poacher's tool. I do not like heavily leaded flies, and I suspect anglers who add weight to the cast of being snigglers. Autumn fish, like their spring counterparts, will come up to your fly to take it and in doing so will hook themselves well. The large fly will fish fairly deeply, without additional weight. The No. 10 slow- or medium-sink line will go down nicely and, with luck and a bit of skill, will fish the fly above the line depth. Those who weight the fly want it to be below the line in depth. Why? I dare say a case might be made out for fishing a heavy fly from a boat in a great dub, especially if the angler cannot cast far. The usual middle and lower Tweed beat, with a combination of wading and boat fishing to offer, responds well to fishing with a longish line, with the line settling nicely down into the stream and the fly following it round but tending to fish up, swimming as it comes round, not dredging. If there is a proper attitude of mind for using this tackle – and I believe that there is – it is summed up in the notion of dwelling on your rod, line and fly as it swings round below you. Let the fly fish at the stream speed. Let the Tweed take your line down and round, and keep your fingers off the line unless you can trust yourself to hold the line gently and sensitively between finger and handle with a yard or more of a loop behind and with some droop between the rod top and the water. Big Tweed fish take line when they seize the fly, and I have sometimes seen five yards going out before the fish turned and was hooked. The notion of dwelling on the tackle as it fishes suggests also that nothing hasty should ever be done in the fishing, particularly in your reaction to the hook. When I see an angler snatching back when he gets a pull, or when he touches a rock, I wonder if he is merely an excitable sort of chap, perhaps a good trout fisher. He should try fishing directly off the reel. Great sport! If I see a Tweed autumn fisher working his deeply sunk line across the stream, snagging the bottom and striking at everything he touches, I am not so charitable as to think he is inexperienced. He is a poacher and I am sorry to say the middle Tweed has its share of them.

If the Tweed is, as some writers have said, part of the great North Sea river, call it the Old Rhine if you will, it might explain why the race of autumn fish it brings in are of such distinctive quality. It might explain why they run so late, becoming in the extreme case winter salmon and not autumn fish. None of us will ever know, but isn't it attractive to speculate that there was a prehistoric river, and that it did breed a race of salmon which ran late and which had all the characteristics of the autumn run in the Tweed today?

Sometimes on the Tweed on a grey autumn day, with the water up and swinging round its glides and pouring through its streams, I feel the primeval quality of the Tweed strongly. It is not a negative feeling at all. It is one of continuity. This continuity, however, has only happened because the owners of Tweed fisheries made it happen. Look at what has happened to the Tyne in Northumberland. It was a salmon river even in recent decades, and I hope will become a salmon river of worth again. The Tweed has the benefit of its own Act and of the dedication of its own commissioners. It has been a fight and it still is a fight to maintain the river at its best. We are seeing the spring fishings improving now, in the mid-eighties, and we are also seeing the autumn fishings equalling the best back-end fishings of the past. Two or three people who know the river well have said to me that the run which came in during the third week of October 1983 was the heaviest run they had ever seen in the Tweed. Clearly, the policies and the management skills of the commissioners are working. One major hurdle remains, however, to ensure the future of the fishings of the river. The anomalous Northumbrian drift-net fishery, which takes Tweed fish by the thousand every season, must be reduced or removed. The main threat to the river is at sea, in the English drift netting (illegal in Scotland) and in illegal sea poaching up and down the coast, from small boats. It is frightening to think that if the Tweed river fishery owners had not fought to control their own fishing, and had not exercised their control with vigilance, sea netting and river poaching might well have eliminated the Tweed as a fishing river years ago. Instead, we have a continuing resource, the value of which is shared by the whole region. As one keen sportsman enjoying the Tweed I am immensely grateful to those who have brought the river into the fourth quarter of the twentieth century with its fishings in such good heart. A river like the Tweed, spring, summer or autumn, is irreplaceable.

25

Big Day at Boleside

There is possibly nothing more boring in angling writing than reading an article which runs, 'I had a nice fourteen-pounder a few casts after starting, then another fine twelve-pounder from the same stream'. Yes, boring, and in one sense unbelievable. An account of a most productive day's salmon fishing in a full angling life which came after the worst spring I had ever had would be doubly unbelievable. Yet it happened that way.

I am lucky enough to share a week at Boleside on Tweed – that lovely beat between the confluence of the Ettrick and the Gala close to Galashiels – and my name came out of a hat for the Thursday and Friday of the first full week of October. This can be a wonderful week on Tweed, always provided the water is

173

right. The Tweed takes its estuary nets off in mid-September and, as if at a signal, the autumn salmon then run in numbers which can range from a trickle to a most impressive and sustained run which can go on for weeks. As they say locally, the October run can turn a hunger into a burst. It did precisely that. I had diligently fished the Tweed on several excellent middle and lower beats from February and had not taken a salmon by the end of September – like many ardent Tweed fishers that year. Then the nets came off and the rains came around the equinox at the end of September and rods up and down the river were in substantial action.

I arrived at the water to find that the river had been too high and coloured to be properly fishable up to Wednesday evening. Fish had been seen going through, but only the odd salmon had been taken. Yet there flowed the Tweed that Thursday morning, 2 feet 7 inches on the gauge, still slightly coloured – bearing that black look, but gliding down the magnificent Boat Pool of Boleside with an almost knowing motion. In salmon-fishing terms, it was just reeking of fish. Not many showed, one here and another there, but fish do not show well in high water.

Yes, I did kill a fish within the first few casts just where you would have predicted it, on the outside of the current where the glide feathers out to form a good stream at a rock headland. What interested me at once was the long, slow take. I was fishing my usual way, with the line lightly held against the butt and with a loop of about two yards hanging behind to give to the fish when I got the draw. The fish was well hooked, but, in the heavy water, had taken all the droop between the rod top and the fly. I should have twigged at once that it was going to be a day of long draws. The next fish seized the fly as it landed and I had only the frustration of a wild pull, but the next came within five minutes, again long and slow in the draw. The young ghillie said that I should perhaps consider striking off the reel and it was exactly the right observation. Sometimes on fast water on the Dee when I am fishing small flies and a floating line I do this, letting the salmon pull directly on to the reel, with a low rod point. It works well there; with a slow-sinking line and a 1¾-inch Brora Waddington, it should work well on Tweed too. It is, in fact, a most exciting way to hook salmon. You do not touch the line at all after casting, but let the fly sweep round under rod control, and it is only when the current slackens off close to your bank that you handline in and recast. Fish which take give you a long, solid pull which makes the reel speak suddenly, or perhaps I should say shriek suddenly. It is astonishingly exciting to feel the take and hear the reel going hard all in the same second. Aren't reel sounds evocative?

I remember years ago being taken carp fishing in Sussex and camping all night by a carp pond. Our rods were set up with ledgered boiled potatoes and we had rigged up bite detectors. After hours and hours of waiting, with a kind of nodding sleep taking over at times, one of the bite detectors went 'ping' and after a lapse of several seconds the reel began to speak, one click at a time, then faster as the carp moved. I have to tell you that I failed to contact that fish when I lifted the rod and struck, but that little series of reel sounds will live with me until I die. The Tweed salmon takes were absolutely different. Wild, large fresh fish tore at the fly and the salmon reel would scream into life giving perhaps five of more yards of line in one fantastic song before the fish turned. In virtually every case on that Boleside day the fish were hooked far back in the mouth, or firmly in the scissors – just the way books say they should be.

Well, not to be too boring about it, we stopped for an early lunch having taken five and lost one. Two other fish had pulled or plucked the fly but had not been hooked. The interesting thing was that I had hardly moved from the rocky point where the first fish had taken. I had the strong impression that the fish were coming to me, and not I moving to the fish. The four other rods came from their various allocated pools on the beat and together we accounted for thirteen fish. Not too bad for lunch time.

My afternoon pool was the Glenmayne Boat Pool and at that height of water it is fished from the boat held tight into the right bank. It looks a very easy pool to fish, but in my view, like many Tweed pools which are boated, it is easy to fish badly. If the boat is hard under the trees, as the Glenmayne boat has to be, it is essential to Spey-cast or roll-cast a fair line to get the fly to work round. Some observers think I am slightly obsessed with getting a good line out, but, after a long time at this business of salmon fishing, I am certain that long lines mean more fish moved and more fish hooked. It is all very well to reach a lie by putting five yards of line out over the stern of a boat. On pools where the boat is held in mid-current this might work tolerably well. But in pools where the fly has to be placed on the other side of a stream, allowed to gain the right depth, and then presented well to fish in the streamy lies, a long line is essential. A line of say twenty or twenty-five yards, perfectly castable with a modern fly rod and easy with my fifteen-foot 'Yorkshire' carbon, allows you to mend and lead the fly at slow fishing speeds over the salmon. This length of line allows you to roll- or Spey-cast effectively, it gives you enough leeway to absorb fast takes, and, if you let the reel speak when the pull comes, it acts as a cushion in the take. This would be true if we were fishing a floating line on the Dee, but it is doubly true when we are fishing a slow-sinking line with a good-size Waddington or tube on Tweed in autumn.

I said I hoped not to bore readers with a succession of hooked fish. Let me just say that when the total for the day reached eight, and I had passed my previous best day ever, I decided to go ashore and let my son, who was looking after a labrador puppy on the bank, fish in my place. I went – and I honestly have never done this before – to Galashiels to buy the champagne. That took fifteen minutes or so, but when I returned my son was playing his first salmon. He had played fish in the past which I had hooked, but this was the real thing. He seemed to be perfectly in control. Can it be in the blood? It did appear to be taking some time, however. The reason was soon clear: it was a magnificent fish, eighteen and a half pounds, the best to fall to my rod that day. Splendid! Champagne was definitely in order.

I went in at the head of the pool again and, to cut me down to size, lost a fish which took hard as I retrieved the fly up the side before recasting, lost another which seemed to take well, and then landed the tenth fish of the day. It was quarter past four. I cannot say the sky was blue in fact, but it felt blue. My mind wandered a bit. We were fishing one pool up from Abbotsford, Sir Walter Scott's home. He was a great fisher and I wondered whether he had in his lifetime there seen an autumn day like this. My musings were interrupted at about that point. A long, heavy draw and a loud scream from the reel reminded me that we were still in business. This time it was not easy. The fish seemed to be immovable. It gave two yards, then took two, and was hard and dour in the fight. 'Maybe it's a big fertiliser bag,' said Len, the head keeper. At times it felt like that, or even like the bedspring I once hooked on the Doon. This bedspring or bag made me work rather hard. I could not get it out of the stream, even after half an hour's fight. It pulled back and tailed down. I began to think it was a fish of quite substantial proportions, yet now and again a tail would show, nothing more, and that did not seem to be the tail of a thirty-pounder. We did have a 28½-pound springer on the Helmsdale one February, however, and I estimated its weight during the fight at seventeen pounds, having seen only the tail. Perhaps history was repeating itself? Then, at the tail of the pool, after it had taken me two hundred yards down without showing, I got the fish into a backwater and with difficulty brought it to the net. It was seventeen and half pounds, exactly the right size for its tail. It was shining fresh yet had fought like a dour, very heavy fish, as red as they might come. It had taken three-quarters of an hour, had messed up most of the pool, and was clearly the last fish of the day. The head keeper asked, since my rod had had eleven, and the all-time rod record for Boleside was thirteen, if I would like to try for a few more minutes, just to see if we could match it. I decided not to. I was replete. I had had the most magnificent big day on water which has fine character, with fish which were fresh, heavy and sporting. What is a record? At that moment, it seemed to be something irrelevant. It was thirty-five years since I had caught my first salmon, and I had never experienced anything like that day. It was what I believe theologians call an existential moment.

The five rods on the beat had brought in twenty-six salmon and satisfaction ruled all round. We drank the champagne, ghillies and rods. The toast was to the big day at Boleside and to our incredible luck in finding a window in the floods.

— 26 —
The Dowie Dens
o' Yarrow

I was washed off the Tweed. There was no ambiguity about it. The river rose that Friday to twelve feet at Kelso. The fishing hut was awash, the boats were at risk, the bridge itself was dangerously near the brown surface of the Tweed. Fishing was off. I had arranged to stay down in Selkirkshire and I hoped to fish the Tweed on Friday and Saturday and on the Monday and Tuesday holiday I thought I might explore the area a little. It was clear, however, that the flood was likely to blot out the Tweed for days and with that in mind I turned my attention to the two tributaries which flow within a few miles of the house I was staying in – the Ettrick and the Yarrow.

If you crossed the Yarrow in summer and didn't notice it, you could be forgiven. It is a slender, beautiful, clear stream with a stony and gravelly bottom, but it is almost hidden between its own bushes, except up near St Mary's Loch, where it wanders through moorlands banks. If you had looked at Yarrow that Monday morning in October, as I did, you would have seen a roaring river of some considerable size. I thought it was worth fishing so, after a few telephone calls and an arrangement to take two day-tickets from a local estate above Selkirk, I found myself on the Yarrow near the village it gives its name to, and even then, three days after the height of the flood, it was very difficult to wade and impossible to cross.

Fishing for salmon on a new river always takes time. Salmon in spate streams like the Yarrow appear like magic as the flood drops and, unless you know where to look for them, you can waste a lot of time and energy trying to find out. This can be doubly trying when the paths have just been washed away by a huge flood. But there are signs. Look for the corner pools. There are always lies there. Look for streams which hold to one bank and dig out a channel leaving a slack margin where fish can rest as they forge upstream. You are looking for running salmon on a spate river like the Yarrow and much of your success lies in seeing fish and predicting where they will take a breather as they fight their way upstream.

I fought my way through bankside bushes for the first day, finding out where the likely pools were, discovering that they were still too high, studying them and cursing whins and brambles. To make matters worse it rained again and I thought the river would never settle. I went back to my holiday house above the Loch of the Lowes, worn out and not very hopeful for day two. I woke to find the weather settled and I was soon driving down the Yarrow valley from St Mary's Loch and at the pool just below the loch where the water authority have a small dam for measuring flow – a pool which many anglers reading this must have seen – I saw, from the car, a salmon leaping. So they were right up the loch. Excellent! They must surely be in the pools near Yarrow too. So I started at the top and fished the top corner pool, which I call Mervyn's father's pool because when Mervyn was keeper there his father had a reputation for taking salmon in autumn from that place. When you don't know the real names of pools on a new river, you can be forgiven for renaming them. Below Mervyn's corner was a fine run in front

179

of a stand of rowan trees. No fish showed, but I smelt them there. I tried Old Bridge run and pool below and decided to drive to the trout farm below and try the well-known corner pool called Tinnis. That pool is magnificent with two feet of water in it, as it had that day. A brawling run slackens as it hits the corner and holds hard to the right bank. It forms glassy reaches on it as it slows down, then it loses its form as it passes a bar of rock on the right bank and dredges a deep, nasty, turbulent eddy. As I dodged through the pine trees on the way to Tinnis Pool I saw the welcome sight of a salmon showing. In the dge of the tail of the turbulence a fish splashed. I waded in under the branches of a tree and roll-cast out to the slacker parts of the headstream.

I was into a fish in three casts – a nice feeling after days of waiting. It fought well in the heavy water then, probably tired out with running, gave up and I netted it out. Seven pounds and, while not a bar of silver, at least not bad for early October. As I fished on, trying the pool down again, I saw first one, then five fish as they entered the pool, showed and, presumably, passed on upstream. Nothing else took me there, although it looked like a perfect taking place.

I went back up to the Old Stone Bridge – the remnants of an ancient bridge with one fine stanchion and one semi-ruined arch. The run above was coming into perfect ply and I decided to fish it down with a slightly smaller orange-and-black Brora fly tied on wire with a fine sharp treble at the tail. I specially mention that because I had, during the day, developed a phobia about the sharpness of my trebles. I started worrying about penetration and I used my little carborundum stone to sharpen two points which seemed dull, but I'm afraid my sharpening seemed to make them duller. This time my treble was perfect, I felt – small and immensely sharp. I fished the run down and at the burn just in front of Lynfoot cottage I had the most sudden, almost vicious take. The slack went, the rod tip bowed and the fish was on – for five seconds. Then this sharpest of trebles came out. It was a nose-hooking job if ever I had experienced one. Nose-hooking of salmon is dreadful. I never trust such a hold and if I see the fly sticking out of the nose as I play the fish I tend to write the fish off. I'll lose it, I say to myself. Well that fish was on and off far quicker than it takes to read two lines of this book.

I fished on, tried the pool again, then went back up to Mervyn's corner.

There, fishing the pool from the left bank, I thought conditions perfect but saw nothing and touched nothing, but the Rowan Trees immediately below looked exceedingly attractive – a long run under the right bank shallowing off into gravel. Great! I swung the fly round, a 1¾-inch Willy Gunn from Brora, orange-red, yellow and black hair. Then, like lightning, a small fish arched over the fly as it came into the shallow and it was on. Was it nose-hooked? I looked anxiously as I played it and there, alarmingly, was the Willie Gun sticking right out of its nose. It must be the most precarious hold in history, I thought. I sweated and fretted a bit but the hooks held and the lively little fish stuck on. So I gained confidence and eventually netted it. The fly was firmly fixed just outside the mouth on the lower jaw right at the point. Inside the mouth was a tell-tale wound where the fish had snatched at the fly and failed to hook itself well. What an incredibly lucky hold I had got with a second hook of the treble! It weighed five pounds, a clean, little, fast fish, but very acceptable indeed. So Yarrow, that river so much sung about in Scott's poems, had yielded me my first two fish from its waters. It was a bonus day, a fine local adventure. The water was right, falling after a flood in autumn. The fish arrived and, even if they were just a little bit given to plucking at the fly, I could not blame them too much because they had added two nice fish from a new water. Yarrow and Ettrick come alive in autumn. So does the Teviot in the valley to the south. Autumn is harvest time there. It felt like that to me, fishing for the first time what Scott calls most appealingly 'the dowie dens o' Yarrow'.

27

Late Encounters on a Sea Trout Loch

A few years ago, the BBC launched a series of films about Scottish game fishing. Do you remember them? There was a phenomenal film about fishing the Findhorn gorges at Logie and there was another with that great master of the art of sea-trout fishing, Charlie McLaren, fishing sea trout in lochs in October – I think the lochs were Clair and Coulin, above Kinlochewe. I had the images of these lochs very much in mind when, in mid-October, I got the chance to fish for three days on a well-known sea-trout loch which I had eyed with envy for some twenty years, but had never launched a boat on.

It is well worth remembering that from about the end of September, or even earlier, some good bits of loch fishing lie untenanted. The guests are away, except for the stalkers, and I have found in some cases that boats are taken off lochs, although there may well be runs of fresh sea trout right through October. I cannot give you names and places, because I only stumble across such opportunities myself, sometimes through a small ad in the papers and sometimes through local tic-tac.

Anyway, I went north and west and on the way it hailed and snowed and I began to doubt my sanity in (a) expecting to launch a boat at all in such weather and (b) finding any self-respecting sea trout (or even a salmon) to come to the fly. The local word, however, was strong. Given any respite in the weather at all, fresh fish, or at least recently arrived fish, would be available in the loch.

The first day was bitterly cold, blowing hard from the north-west. Luckily our boat was tucked away into a bay sheltered somewhat from the gusts and, after some thought, we decided it was worth a try. Each of us mounted our carbon rods. Mine is the heavy-duty model, well able to handle salmon or sea trout, if slightly hard on the wrist over long, windy days. I would always mount a cast of large wet flies, but when the wind is high I go for the largest, fuzziest and bulkiest flies in my box. My friend, who is a first-class fly tier and fisher, chose a size 8 heavily dressed Poacher and, on the bob, a similar size of Black Zulu. He had tied in triple hackles to his flies, making the palmer-style bodies very bushy and thick. I didn't have exactly what I wanted in my box, but I did find a good Soldier Palmer for the bob and I tried various flies on the tail, including the fail-me-not Dark Mackerel.

In the gale-force winds which not only raised a wave and a ripple but eventually raised scud, darkening and flattening of the ripple in patches, conditions were not comfortable and were not good. If you raised your eyes from the loch, the tops of the hills were white down to 1500 feet – and they stayed that way. Stags roared on both sides of the loch. There were some scenic compensations for being cold and locally thought to be soft in the head.

During our first drift I rose some finnock which I failed to hook, and my companion rose twice and got into a splendid sea trout of three or four pounds which I was sure was in the bag until it decided to run up wind, leaving us blowing down wind and distancing ourselves from it. I pulled us round and made some ground, took a couple of pictures, and got the net ready. I saw the fish clearly twice, but suddenly, without any drama, the hooks came out. It was the only fish we managed to get during the day, save for three good finnock. We were blown off the loch shortly after that and, although we pottered on the river, the wind there did not help fishing at all.

It was astonishing to wake up the next day and find October up to its tricks. It was totally still. The loch was like a mirror reflecting the hills in magnificent autumn colours. Stags roared everywhere as we motored up to the head and waited for a midday or afternoon wind. It usually happens in the west. I have been becalmed at lunch time and buffeted by a stiff wind by two o'clock. We took an early lunch and I got my big flies ready, despite the calm conditions. Then it came, steady and stiffening, and I was starting out on the first drift of the day. I had a great size 6 long-shank Black Pennell on the tail and I had my big Soldier Palmer above it. Right away I had a flurry of finnock, one of them about a pound. Great! It might be going to happen.

It did, but it was on quite another drift half an hour later. After another finnock my friend bent his rod into a splendid fish and this time there was no doubt. It was well hooked on the Poacher. It weighed, we estimated, about three and a half pounds. He had his turn at finnock sport too, returning some small fish, then as we drifted across the weeds I had the most lovely flash to my flies at the extremity of my cast and was into a strong fish which fought tenaciously before finally coming to the net. When it was laid alongside my friend's fish it seemed to be a couple of ounces heavier, if slightly more coloured. When we got home, we weighed both, found that each was actually three and a quarter pounds, with mine possibly half an ounce lighter than his. A fine pair of sea trout and well worth the cold hands (we were both wearing every jersey we could find and we had mittens on). My fish so wanted the great Black Pennell dressed on its long, low-water single hook that it practically swallowed it and was hooked in the rays of the vomer.

The third day repeated the uncertainties of the one before. There was no wind at all for two hours, then a puff, then calm, before a later afternoon breeze set in and made fly-fishing possible. We got into finnock, and then my colleague began to move better fish (I suspect two of them were salmon). He felt them, but did not hook them. What would we do? We thought of

184

the dap and he tried that, moving three other excellent fish but not touching them. Isn't that typical of the dap? You move them, and see them, and wonder why the hooks are not going in. In fact it is the fly that isn't being taken. Fish show to the dap readily, are excited by it, but often miss it – I believe intentionally. Wet fly can do well while this is going on, but not that day. We were blank for the afternoon, except for under-sized finnock which I returned, and a fish of a pound and a quarter taken by my friend.

Looking back on this late-autumn loch foray, we were really rather pleased with it. It was cold, patchy, frustrating, yet productive. All the time we felt sure that, given a few days of warmer weather, we could have scored. The fish were there, but they would only move in small periods of activity. The salmon were also there, and some of them were fairly fresh. They would show, but not take, unless some of our false rises were salmon rolling to the fly. But it had all the elements of magnificence in it. The hills never looked so good with their snow tops, the stags were loud and romantic (and some were romantically shot while we were there), and the fish had not quite forgotten the sport of the summer. Yes, it was good enough to help you forget the hailstorms and to make it seem worth while to fish for a typically summer fish, the sea trout, in the garb of the spring-salmon fisher.

28

The St Andrew's Day
Event

The Tweed is not unique in remaining open for rod fishing until
the end of November. A scattering of other Scottish rivers enjoy
this extended season, including the Nith. The Tweed, however,
so justifies this late closing of its rod fishings that it virtually
classifies itself as a winter river. The late-autumn runs of
November are often postponed until the last days of the month,
or, in periods of low water, until mid-December. Then, heavy,
fresh November fish, mixed with small shining late runners,
merge with a scattering of springers. The winter fishing, which I
would love to try but cannot because the river is closed, might

produce some surprising results. I have often found myself shooting on the banks of middle Tweed, or taking a winter walk beside the river, and seeing excellent water running with fish showing – some kelts and, who knows, some fresh fish. During its short winter, Tweed hints at its secret runs. Our unforgettable St Andrew's Day event in 1982 was a preview of what has been described to me as the most prolific winter the Tweed has had in living memory.

I call it the St Andrew's Day event, but I must begin the story the day before, on the second last day of the Tweed season, 29 November. We had had an unbearable series of floods on the river right through October and November. There was gnashing of teeth and much misery among regular tenants of the river. I know the feeling well. Word comes from the river that it is running at three feet and, if the rain would just slacken, sir, it would fine off nicely for next Monday. But the rain comes again, up goes the level, down comes the colour, and yet another week of the marvellous autumn fishings is virtually wiped out. I had shared in this frustration and I could hardly believe my luck when my colleague who had organised the fishing on Lower Floors for the last two days of the season, Monday 29 and Tuesday 30 November, phoned to say that things looked promising. I scurried down to the river on the Sunday and after the long series of brown floods I could hardly believe my eyes. The river was running clear, a little over two feet, and if ever there was a perfect water this was it.

When we arrived at the hut to start the day, there was a whiff of excitement, masked by a caution which only Tweed boatmen can command. Yes, the water looked right, but few fish were showing. I almost believed it, but all my vibrations said salmon and I took the conservatism of the boatmen to be a product of having seen too many good salmon days and having suffered so many floods. I tied on my fly and was given my marching orders to go and fish the Gauge Pool just below the hut, to stay there until about half past eleven, and then to go down to the large Garden Pool and the Putt and try my fly there.

The Gauge has a great tree at its head and a certain amount of Spey-casting helps to pass its trailing branches, but for most of its length the pool is backed by a steep grassy bank clear of obstructions. I thought that the water at the tree was rather fast

187

so on about my fourth cast I moved two yards downstream and as the fly came round I was firmly into a salmon, just over sixteen pounds. Upstream on the Island I could see Robert Bomford into a fish, which was netted for him. I moved down a further two yards and was into another and about that time I realised that this was no ordinary day. The river was packed with fish, nearly all cocks and nearly all very fresh. I had four out of the Gauge before half past eleven and I saw Bert Morris into several before I walked down to the Garden Pool feeling that the Tweed not only did not owe me anything more for the day but had redeemed itself after an autumn of frustration. I had three more down below before returning with the other rods for lunch. We had a count – nineteen fish between us – took a picture, sat like well regulated chaps and actualy ate lunch while David Young, our host, organised the afternoon's fishing. Everybody had killed fish and everybody knew this eve of St Andrew's Day was quite out of the ordinary.

The afternoon was short but I managed to add three to my own total, getting one from under the branches of the great tree on the Gauge, and two more from the Ferry Pool above, which I thought was a magnificent piece of water at that height. A fast spread-out headstream concentrates to form a run hard in to the right bank which forms lies above and below a reinforced promontory. I was boated down the pool and held my breath a bit as I passed over the best lies and took nothing. I had to wait until the last draw-off of the pool, where it changes direction to flow round a rocky ledge – which that day was an island – and where running fish were seen throughout the whole time I was fishing. I retraced my steps and tried the main run again, and this time, off the reinforced point, took my tenth fish of the day.

The whole day produced thirty salmon to four rods. Their total weight was 376 lb 12 oz. Two were over twenty pounds, either were between fifteen and twenty pounds, thirteen were between ten and fifteen pounds and the remainder were in that category of shining small fish which the Tweed has a genius for producing in late autumn and early spring. One of the fish was an undoubted springer of fifteen pounds. We later verified that it was in fact in this class and would not have spawned until autumn 1983. Almost all the fish were clean run, and there were lice on several. Most of the bag was cock fish and we took no gravid hens – a rule we had set ourselves at the beginning of the day. We did not need to apply it. There appeared to be no red fish in the beat.

That was the eve of St Andrew's Day. We were in amazingly optimistic mood for the day itself. The water had fallen a couple of inches, but was still in splendid ply. Fish were running through as we tackled up and we were rapidly on our allocated pools. It was what any angler would have called a good day. We killed twenty-two fish between us, but it seemed a day of steady sport rather than spectacular bursts. I shall not forget one fish of twenty and a half pounds which seized my fly beside the Island run and did so with such force on the dangle that it seemed to want to take my arm off too. It took while I was handlining the fly up the gentle water and I had the impression that it was a fish which had shown in the fast water and had followed the fly very quickly and swirled on it with great force as I handlined the fly back for recasting. It was a very difficult fish to get to the net. Also, I thought, it must surely be badly hooked, having taken like that. It was, it turned out, very firmly hooked indeed and it fought hard and long. It was a slightly dark cock with a good kype and I was well down from the island before I managed to get it in.

The second day proved to be steady, rather than spectacular, as I have said, but one particularly interesting piece of fishing stays vividly in my memory. In the afternoon I was sent to the Garden and the Putt to fish it by wading. That long, slowish pool forms a glide down below the wall of the garden on the Kelso bank and broadens to form a very wide glide for a hundred yards or so down beside the little park where Kelso people sit and watch the fishing, or walk their dogs. On this glide, fish were head-and-tailing, as usual, just out of reach of my deepest wade and my best St Andrew's Day cast. In the fairly heavy water still running, I found myself up to the waist in the Tweed and bouncing a little as I fished a long sinking line slowly round below me.

I used the technique I have mentioned elsewhere in this book, letting the fly swing round under the influence of the current, and leaving the reel free to react to any takes. It was tremendous. The long cast, the steadily swinging line with the fly perhaps three feet down and the anticipation of pulls created a marvellous tension. When the pull came, the reel would speak and line would go off by the yard until the fish stopped and I was able to raise the rod and start the fight. In these conditions, it was again clear that salmon will often take a fly and turn downstream with it, darting away and turning with their prize several yards below. By that time, of course, they have firmly hooked themselves against the weight of the line. I did nothing, except let the reel speak. These fish were very well hooked, as I believe most fish struck from the reel like this are.

I did lose one, and I think it was my only loss for the two days. It was at least my only loss after a fight, for, on productive days like these, plucks and pulls happened. This was, I believe, the biggest fish of the two days. I had the reel go and was into him and knew from the start that he was in a different class. That fish moved where and when it felt like it. In wide open water like the tail of the Garden he could go where he would, up to a hundred yards or more. Several times he took a lot of line and then, obligingly, came back, but on each occasion I felt that it was his fight and not mine. I fought him for quite some time and then found I was more and more in control. But he was very hard to bring to the top. When I did get him up I saw a great high back, I had a glimpse of a large head with a big kype, and as he turned away a tail like a shovel showed. I had to net him out there in the pool and it was difficult. There was nothing the boat could do to help me. Nor did I want it. I managed to get the fish quite close to me on the surface and saw that its power came from its comparative shortness and great depth. It was one of those high-backed, thick cock fish which are devils to get to the net. I was alone, well out in the glide, and I judged that I had to net the fish there. I got the Gye net off, and made two attempts, but each time the fish drifted down with the current and there was no way I could pull it up to be netted. Doing that would certainly put dreadful pressure on the hook-hold and I would never attempt it. I decided to fight the fish round again, and go further downstream, although the water was deepening a bit. I got the fish round, got his head up and tried the drift, and as I did so the hooks came out and, with a final wallow, he slipped into the depths. I cannot say accurately what that fish might have weighed. It was not huge. It was a typical fairly large Tweed autumn fish. It may have run well into the twenties, or it may have shown in the net that its strength outclassed its weight. It was certainly a very powerfully built salmon. What I remember most, however, is the excellent take and the fight which followed. It was a most sporting fish, and it won.

I had been told that the day's fishing would finish at about the time the lights of Kelso came on. They did so at about quarter past four and, in a rather theatrical way, marked the end of the scene that St Andrew's Day and the end of a remarkable season. I was still waist-deep in the glide when the orange sodium lights came on and, as I would normally do, I fished a couple of last casts for luck as they got the boat in above me and began tying up. As a marvellous final gesture, I had a pull in the gloom and a seven-pounder, as fresh as any fish could be, came to the fly and was netted in behind the fence where the boat is tied. That turned out to be the twenty-second fish of the day for the four rods. It had been a slightly quieter day, but only in the way comparatives have of being misleading.

There is something slightly awkward in writing about fishing like this. Lots of first-class salmon fishers hope all their lives to get among fresh salmon like this and not many do. It was my own thirty-seventh season of salmon fishing and I had never experienced anything like those two days, except, ironically, the two big days at Boleside, a few weeks before, in the same weird season, 1982. I had enjoyed, as the Irish might say, the worst season of my fishing life up to the end of August of that year. I had had classical blanks on the Helmsdale, Dee, Tweed and Tay in the spring. I had failed to bring anything to the net in the Spey, although I had lost fish twice. It was a disaster. Then quite suddenly in late summer I had two good days on the Lochy, two excellent days on the Shiel a week later, then a fantastic day of ten followed by a splendid day of five on Boleside. After that, I had the lull everybody endured throughout the flooded Tweed autumn and was lucky enough to land seventeen fish in the two days I have just described as the St Andrew's Day event on Lower Floors.

I don't know how best to describe my feelings, looking back fifteen months to that strange autumn of 1982. I know I floated through the sparse spring of 1983 on the lift the previous autumn had given me and when our turn came again to fish Boleside in late September and we found low water and very poor fishing conditions I felt the river owed me nothing. When it came to fishing Lower Floors again in the vastly different conditions of the end of November 1983, when low, stale water prevailed, and this time, four rods fished three days for only five red cock fish, none of them above eleven pounds, I again felt the beat owed me nothing. I hope St Andrew has not done for me by making me blasé, as the dictionary has it 'with no more taste for enjoyment having been spoiled by over indulgence'. Not a bit of it. I know what salmon fishing is like. It is usually hard work for occasional reward. St Andrew's Day events, even under the influence of that lucky fisherman, are very rare indeed.